Joseph L. Patten

Manual of Needlework

Teaching how to do Kensington, Applique, Cretonne, Roman,

Cross-stitch...

Joseph L. Patten

Manual of Needlework

Teaching how to do Kensington, Applique, Cretonne, Roman, Cross-stitch...

ISBN/EAN: 9783337047122

Printed in Europe, USA, Canada, Australia, Japan

Cover: Foto ©Andreas Hilbeck / pixelio.de

More available books at **www.hansebooks.com**

MANUAL OF NEEDLEWORK.

TEACHING HOW TO DO

KENSINGTON, APPLIQUE, CRETONNE, ROMAN, CROSS-STITCH, OUTLINE AND OTHER EMBROIDERIES.

HOW TO MAKE

HONITON, MODERN POINT AND MACRAME LACE, DARNED NET, &c.

ALSO,

GIVES INSTRUCTION IN KNITTING, CROCHETING, TATTING, RUG MAKING, &c.

With numerous directions for making many articles of Home and Personal Adornment.

PROFUSELY ILLUSTRATED.

NEW YORK:
PATTEN PUBLISHING COMPANY,
47 BARCLAY STREET.
1883.

NEEDLEWORK.

There cannot be too much said in favor of this branch of female education. Needlework is most essentially feminine, and the great importance of early training, in the art of plain needlework cannot be overestimated. No young girl should be allowed to reach womanhood without at least mastering the needle sufficiently to keep in order her own wardrobe, thus training her hands to activity and making preparation for future home usefulness.

Fancy or decorative needlework is at present engrossing the female mind to a considerable degree, and supposing the first rudiments to have already been taught, the object of this little book is to teach the use of the needle in the various kinds of work, which the necessities of housekeeping and requirements of tasteful home decoration may demand.

COTTON EMBROIDERY

Enters very largely into the ornamentation of undergarments, as well as being much used for trimming linen and cambric dresses, and children's suits, therefore this shall receive our first attention.

BUTTON HOLE STITCH

Is of first importance, as it is always used to edge cotton embroidery. The point or scallop is first very carefully traced or stamped upon the material to be embroidered, after which two rows of stitches should be run in, to define both upper and under edge of the point or scallop. It is well then to fill in between these threads with long loose stitches of cotton, not only to add to the strength and durability of the work, but to give it a heavy raised appearance when finished. (Cut No. 2.)

It will be seen by reference to the cuts 1 and 2, that the needle should pass through just at the edge of the top thread, coming

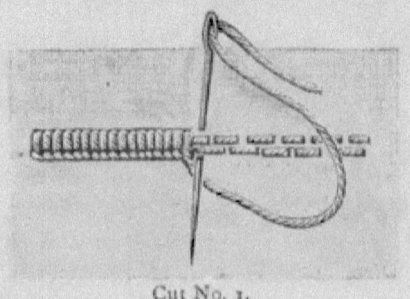

Cut No. 1.

out just under the lower line or thread, while the cotton is held by the left thumb a little to the right of where the needle is to come

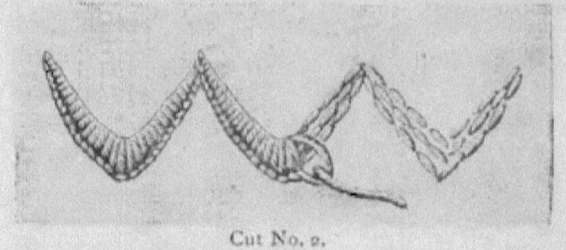

Cut No. 2.

through, so that as the needle and thread is drawn up, a loop is formed which fastens itself.

SATIN STITCH.

All leaves and flowers, both in cotton and silk embroidery are worked in this stitch. The edges of the leaf or flower should be

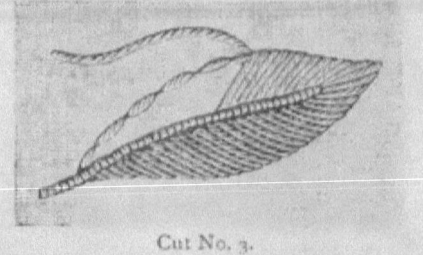

Cut No. 3.

run round, closely following the stamped pattern, then with a coarse embroidery cotton fill the space with long loose stitches, lengthwise of the leaf or petal, or in a contrary direction from the stitches which are to cover them. After this is done, the stitches should be put in over and over, laying closely side by side, and the defining line of the pattern very carefully followed. Small leaves should be worked from the center outward and *all* leaves from the veining out toward the points. (Cut No. 3.)

The veining should be thus marked by the work or the meeting of the satin stitches. Flowers are worked from the center outward, and each petal separately.

SPOT STITCH

Is merely a short back stitch, and is used sometimes in filling in parts of leaves, to give variety to the work. Larger dots are run round with cotton, and after being filled in, by passing the cotton across the circle two or three times, the stitches are then worked in the opposite direction, one laying closely by the side of the other, as in satin stitch.

OPEN WORK EMBROIDERY OR EYELET HOLES.

The design is first stamped, and then the lines are all run round with cotton or floss. If a leaf, it is then slashed with the scissors,

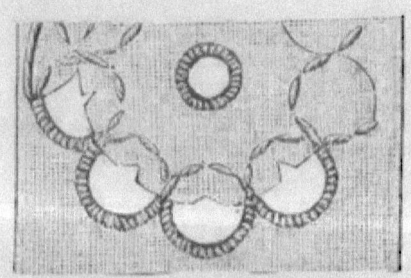

Cut No. 4.

and the material drawn or tucked under, or back, to where the leaf is defined, then carefully sewed over and over, the stitches being close together. If an eyelet only is to be made, a stilletto pierced through the material will be all that is necessary, working over and over, as before stated. Be careful that the needle is brought up each time just where the eyelet or leaf is defined, as the evenness of the work depends wholly on this. (Cut No. 4.)

WHEEL STITCH.

Sometimes a wheel is used to give variety to work. It is first run round, then carefully cut out with a pair of fine scissors, do not cut to the extreme size you wish to make your wheel, but leave a little margin to turn back under, to make the work firm. The space is now filled in evenly with long threads passing back and forth from side to side, and knotted in the center. The edge of

Cut No. 5.

Cut No. 6.

the wheel is then carefully sewed over and over, or finely button-hole stitched. There are a great many designs for wheels, and considerable practice is required to work them, but when these stitches are once mastered a person can do all the different varieties of cotton embroidery.

HERRING BONE STITCH.

This stitch is much used in joining the seams of flannel, so they shall be flat, one breadth overlapping the other. It is used also for decorating tidies, towels, etc., and when one kind of fabric is to be applied to another in fancy work, it makes a very effective stitch. It is also used in ornamenting aprons and other children's garments, where it is not desirable to spend time for embroidery. It is done by sewing backwards and alternating loops of loose button-hole stitch. The cut will give a better idea than any description could possibly do. (See cut No. 6.)

CHAIN STITCH.

This stitch is very useful in a variety of ways. It is used for fastening the edges of *applique* work, for embroidery on flannel, for table covers, stitching in braiding patterns, with colored floss or silk, and may be used on linen and children's clothes, using floss or cotton of a contrasting color. Braiding patterns worked in chain stitch, in colored cotton, will wash and wear better than the braid which is so much used, and takes very little more time to accomplish.

This stitch (see cut No. 7) is formed by a loop made first upon the upper side of the material, and the needle passed up through, se-

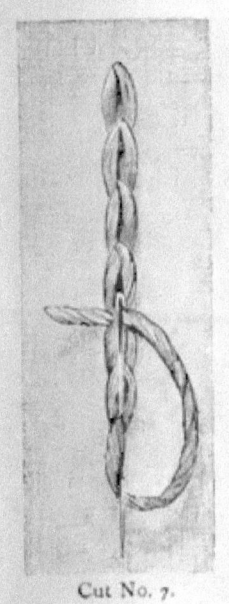
Cut No. 7.

Cut No. 8.

curing the loop. The needle is then passed down very near where it was drawn up, the left thumb holding the thread so it cannot be wholly drawn back, a stitch is taken towards you and each time the loop is left around the needle, forming a link in the chain stitch. Double Chain Stitch is done much the same, only the thread is twisted. (See cut 8.)

KNOT STITCH.

The centers of flowers are usually made in this stitch, in all kinds of fancy embroidery. To form the knot, bring the needle up through the material at the place where you wish to place the knot;

wind the silk twice around the needle and then put the needle back in precisely the place where it has come up. Draw the silk

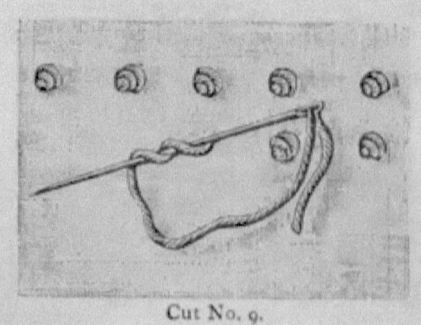

Cut No. 9.

through carefully, to avoid tangling, and the twist thus formed becomes a knot. (Cut 9.)

BLANKET STITCH

Is used for finishing the edges of blankets, the edges of chair or table scarfs, valances for windows or mantels. It is a button-hole stitch in reality and made in fanciful designs, by sloping the needle to the right and left, or by making two or more stitches close together, then leaving a space between, and so on. It is also very

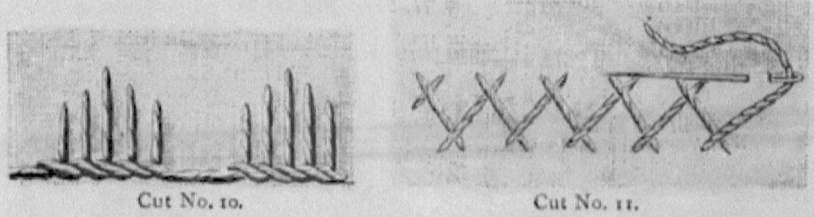

Cut No. 10.   Cut No. 11.

pretty in effect to work a second row over the first row with a different shade or color of silk.

This stitch will be found useful for many purposes, as it makes firm an edge when material of another kind is to be applied. (See cut No. 10.)

The stitch, as seen in cut No. 11, is one used for joining the edges of flannel and for many uses in fancy needle-work.

HEM STITCHING.

Hem Stitch is used for handkerchiefs, linen collars and cuffs, the edges of fine ruffles, etc., etc. A few threads are first drawn out where the hem is to be fastened down. The drawn threads are then separated with the needle, taking up each time about the same num-

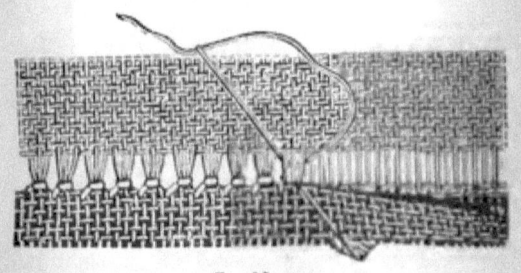

Cut No 12.

ber of threads to keep the work even, and the stitch taken twice in the same place; this secures the stitch, and forms the little open space which gives the ornamental finish to an otherwise plain hem. An examination of the cut, and a little ingenuity, will enable one to make this stitch better than written instructions could possibly do. (See cut No. 12.)

RAILWAY STITCH.

Called thus because so rapidly worked, is very pretty for wheat ears (cut 13), and in many other ways it can be introduced, making very effective work. No running out is necessary; the tracing being done, the needle is placed exactly through the two parts of the tracing that the stitch is to cover, then the cotton or silk is twisted round the needle, as in Knot Stitch, as many times as is required to cover the space or stitch. In the cut given it is wound round ten times; the needle is then pulled through the work and that stitch is complete.

FEATHER (OR CORAL) STITCH.

This stitch which is illustrated by cuts No. 14 and 15, is found useful in many kinds of fancy needlework, besides being used in joining the seams of flannel, a description is unnecessary as the cuts fully explain the manner of forming the stitch.

MANUAL OF NEEDLEWORK.

BARDEN STITCH

Is a flat conching used much in silk embroideries. It is useful in *applique* embroidery, and is worked by laying down a line of *filloselle*, to secure which a thread of another color should be brought up from the back of the material on one side the *filloselle*

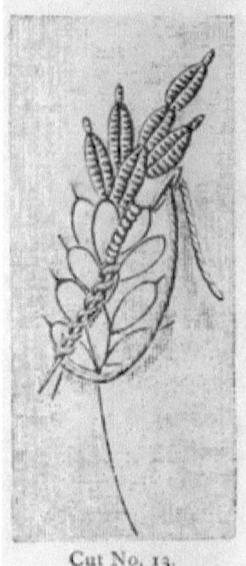

Cut No. 13.

Cut No. 14.

Cut No. 15.

and carried back on the other. The stitches which secure the *filloselle* should be perfectly equal in their distances from each other. Gold cords, and edging cords of all kinds are best fastened down in the same way, using fine sewing silk to fasten them on with. When the outline is finished, a small hole should be pierced with a stiletto in the material, and the cord cut off and passed through on the other side where it is fastened.

KENSINGTON NEEDLEWORK,
OR CREWEL WORK.

This style of embroidery is at present taking rank as one of the most popular and pleasing forms of fancy needlework. It is easy of execution, so that a mere novice in embroidery may do very pretty and artistic work, while really beautiful works of art are sometimes produced by experts. Very much of course depends upon individual taste in this, as in all kinds of fancy work. It has been called by some, "needle painting," and an excellent way to shade in the different colors of this embroidery, is to copy the natural flower or leaf as in painting with the brush, or to take a painting or fine chromo lithograph, and copy exactly the shading; this is perhaps easier for an amateur than copying direct from nature.

MATERIAL.

The crewel which is used in this work, is a strong two threaded woolen yarn, differing materially from zephyr and other yarns in texture and twist. It is made in all the soft beautiful colors not found in other yarns, which render it particularly suitable for the proper imitation of the soft blending tints of natural leaves and flowers. There is also a silk, called *filloselle*, or filling floss, which introduced into the shading of the leaves or flowers gives a much richer and finer effect. Two or three threads of the *filloselle* are used, when in conjunction with the crewel, which makes about the same sized thread. This floss should not be used on cotton goods, but only on felts, plushes, satins, etc., etc.

The work may either be done in a frame, or in the hand. Nearly all embroidery, on work of large size, can be more neatly worked in a frame, and where the work is too long to be placed in a frame at once, it can be put in one section at a time.

In use, the frame rests upon the lap of the worker, the left arm is placed inside, so that the arm rests upon the bottom board. The downward stitch is taken with the right hand, and the upward stitch taken with the left hand, so that the left hand is always kept below, while the right hand is above the work. Many persons find it a little slower to use the left hand in this way, but practice will overcome any such difficulty.

When working with silks or flosses, the hands should be kept smooth and free from rings upon which the silk is apt to become entangled.

Some use the floss wholly in executing small designs upon satin or plush, as it makes finer work, but for large pieces of work, the crewel with an occasional strong light thrown in with silk is quite as effective.

If one is situated so they cannot obtain a frame ready made, almost any carpenter can construct one. It should be arranged with holes at each end of the sides which can be kept secure with pegs. A strip of cotton cloth should be fastened by small nails to the frame, and the work secured by long stitches to this cloth. If satin or any other material is used, which will fray easily, a piece of muslin should be carefully basted all over the edge of the material, and then attached by that to the frame.

THE STITCHES AND MODE OF WORKING.

The stitch itself is exceedingly simple, and the least mechanical of all the stitches used in fancy work.

Cut No. 16.   Cut No. 17.

A knot being made in the worsted it is brought from the under side of the material to the surface ; the needle is then passed back again from the upper side, leaving the stitch a quarter of an inch, more or less, on the upper side.

The length of the stitches should be left entirely to the judgment of the worker, who will make them longer or shorter, according to the space to be covered, or the texture of the material wrought upon. The stitches should be smoothly and evenly laid and should, when done, resemble the woof of satin, but as will be seen by examination of the cuts, No. 18 and No. 19, the stitches

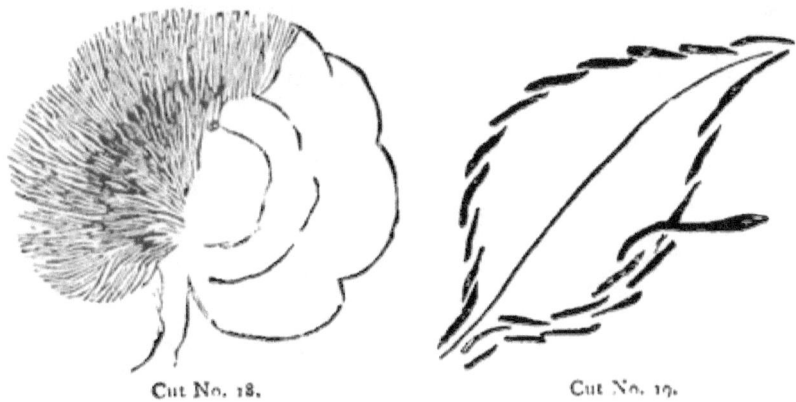

Cut No. 18.　　　　　　　Cut No. 19.

are not to be laid evenly side by side and of equal lengths, like satin embroidery, but more like the hatching, in water-color drawing, one line dove-tailing into another, so that no abrupt terminations are seen.

The outline of the work should first be covered; begin at the lower end of the stalk or flower, and work on until the outline is crossed by a leaf, or terminates in a flower, then pass the needle to the other side and work back again to the lower end : then work another line of stitches *inside* of the outline, until the stalk is filled up. The outline of the design should always be evenly and closely followed, but the interior of the petal or leaf must be filled in, according to the shape. (Cut No. 21).

The stalk of a flower should never be worked *across*, but invariably lengthways. In shading much depends upon the taste of the worker; those who have a knowledge of drawing and coloring will find it very easy to produce fine effects in this work. The principal fault to guard against is stiffness, for while Crewel designs are hardly expected to be in every respect true to nature, yet they should never have that set appearance which is found in cotton embroidery, therefore preserve as far as possible the prominent characteristics of the plant or flower which you are trying to imitate.

After the work is finished and taken from the frame, it generally

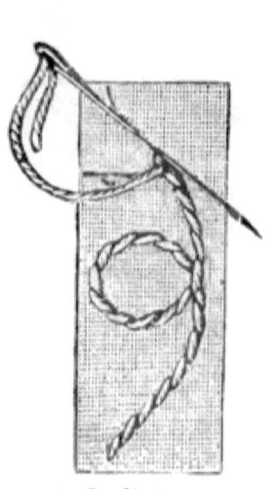

Cut No. 20.

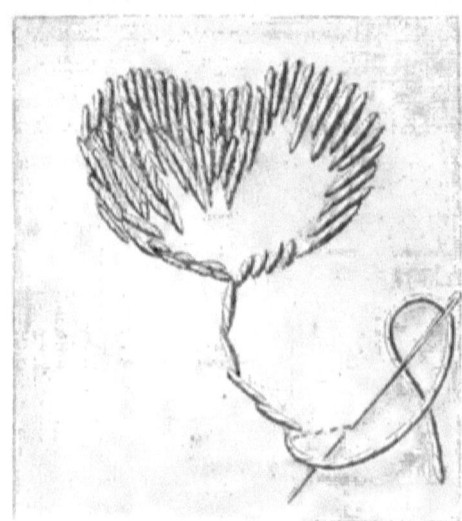

Cut No. 21.

appears somewhat drawn or puckered. This is remedied by stretching the work, tight and smooth, face downward on an ironing table, after which place a damp cloth over the surface of the work, and run a hot iron over it, when it has been thus steamed, run the iron over it until it is perfectly dry, and the work will be found smooth and even.

ARRASENE EMBROIDERY.

A new material for artistic embroidery, called Arrasene, has recently been introduced, which is likely to supersede Filloselle and Crewels in all kinds of bold designs in decorative needlework. It is a kind of fine chenile, and comes in both silk and wool, in all the beautiful varieties of color necessary for shading. It is suitable thus not only for all kinds of home decoration, but also for embroidering articles of wearing apparel, and it is equally suitable for the finest fabrics, as well as the cheaper materials used in needlework.

It is very easy to work, and much more rapidly done than the crewel work, although much the same stitch is required, cording or stem-stitch being about the best stitch to use, with this difference, that the stitch should be about a quarter of an inch on the surface of the material, and a much shorter stitch used underneath, which is not only more economical in the use of the Arrasene, but also brings the fibres closer together on the work, giving a richer appearance to it when finished. Sometimes in smaller flowers on velvet,

Cut No. 22.

or plush, it is sewed upon the surface without being drawn through. A chenile or rug needle should be used, with an eye large enough to let the thread pass through without displacing the fibre, and also that the fibre should not be injured in passing through the material.

It is not necessary to use a frame in working small designs, but larger ones are more easily thus kept in place. If the work becomes drawn in working, it can be straightened by first covering a board with a wet cloth, and then firmly pinning the work to the board, with the wrong side down, over the wet cloth, and allowing it to remain until the cloth is perfectly dry; this takes out the irregularities, and leaves the work smooth.

We have recently seen some window lambrequins, or valances,

worked in Arrasene; the material was olive sateen, with a border of fleur de lis, tulips, lilacs, jonquils, ferns, and grasses. Below the work was a band of maroon plush, edged with fringe corresponding in color. All these flowers, it will be noticed, are bold in design, and the effect of color, light, and shade was very fine.

A NEW STITCH

Has recently been introduced into art embroidery, which is called Plush Stitch. By its use Sumach, Cockscomb, Golden Rod, Princess Feather, Love-Lies-Bleeding, and similar flowers which before could only be very imperfectly represented, can now be closely imitated both in texture and coloring.

To work it, the outline of the flower should be first filled up with large French knots of the prevailing color; (see cut No. 9), then, using button-hole twist, bring the needle up *between* the knots, lay a doubled strand of filling floss on the face of the work, against the needle; take the needle back, after crossing the floss, at about the same place it came up, so that when the needle is drawn down, the stitch has caught the filling silk about a quarter of an inch from its end; draw the stitch tightly, and the filling silk will spring up straight, then clip off with a pair of sharp scissors, and one stitch is completed; repeat until the knots in the background are *nearly* covered. It is not easy to describe, but a little practice and judgement in the clipping, will produce very charming effects, much resembling the real flower. Care should be taken that the stitches do not *entirely* cover the knots, but only partially, as too great closeness of the stitches is apt to give a heavy appearance to the work when finished.

In the Cockscomb, the upper part, or comb, should be worked with a rich velvety crimson; the stitches should be very close, and clipped quite *long*, the convolutions of the comb being represented by using three shades of crimson. The lower part from the stem up to the comb, shows the green seeds, this is imitated by making the knots of dead green crewel, and a few of the plush stitches interspersed, using a single thread of the floss made of both red and green. Clip these a little closer than the comb itself, and use the red more freely as it approaches the comb.

OUTLINE WORK

Is a popular work at present. It is suitable for many things, but especially in favor for splashers, doylies, and the ends of towels, etc., using for this purpose red or black cotton only. Some prefer to

Cut No. 23.

work in color, and for such, there is a kind of etching silk which comes expressly for the work and will stand washing—the plain colors are, however, greatly preferable.

The stitch used is simply a stem or outline stitch. (Cuts 22 and 23.)

CRETONNE EMBROIDERY

Is similar to Applique, only instead of cutting out designs of cloth or velvet, the designs are cut from cretonne and sateen such as is used for upholstering. The pattern should be cut out with a fine pair of scissors ; lay them face downward and paste carefully with very fine gum arabic, or a little starch, then lay upon the fabric, where you have previously arranged to place them, and the gum or starch will keep them in place. Soft floss silk is the best for cretonne edges, and the work must be carefully done in close fine satin stitch, blending with color the silk and cretonne.

CANVAS WORK

In all its varieties is so common that description is unnecessary. We give diagrams of the most common stitches used, such as

Cut No. 24.

Cut No. 25.

single and cross stitch, cuts 24 and 25 ; also a few cuts illustrating fancy borders, corners, etc., used in this work.

Cuts 29 and 30 are stitches often used in various kinds of fancy work.

SPANISH LACE WORK.

A very pretty style of embroidery is that of basting upon the edge of a lambrequin of satin or plush, a piece of Spanish lace of a well-defined pattern of flowers and leaves, and then working over the pattern with bright colors of embroidery silk, in satin stitch, in some places covering *wholly* the pattern, and other parts only partially.

Both black and white lace are used, and with very good effect, according to the color of the material used for the foundation.

BEAD EMBROIDERY

Is one of the novelties in decorative needlework.

Colored metal beads are made the same as cut steel, and colored with transparent lacquer, allowing the metallic luster of the bead to show through. They produce very pleasing effects when used on material such as satin or plush.

In using them a stitch much like the crewel stitch is used, as many beads being strung on at each stitch as is necessary for the length of stitch desired. As the colors can be varied with each stitch, the work can be very prettily shaded.

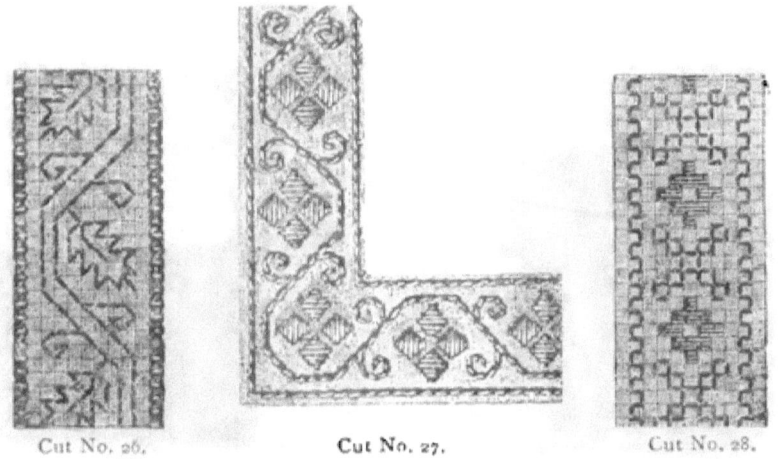

Cut No. 26.   Cut No. 27.   Cut No. 28.

LATTICE-WORK EMBROIDERY.

A novelty in artistic needlework has just appeared, called Lattice-work Embroidery. It is used for table-scarfs as a whole, or in borders, also for the borders of portierres, lambrequins, etc. It receives its name from the manner in which it is worked.

It is treated thus: Place a fine gold cord, or a thread of pale yellow silk in Borden stitch, diagonally, about one inch apart, across the material to be decorated, then place the threads in the opposite direction which covers the material in diagonal squares. A design is then stamped over these squares, of some trailing pattern, such as clematis, woodbine, etc. (or a spray of wild roses, or dogwood, is also very pretty), and this is worked in crewel or *filloselle* embroidery. When it is completed, it has the effect of a vine or shrub creeping over lattice-work.

It is very pretty worked the same way on blue felt or plush, giving the effect of sky. Linen worked in this way, with the lattice-work in olive silk, and a spray of woodbine in bright colors trailing over it, edged with a fringe for tidies, etc., is also very pretty.

WORKING MATERIAL.

There are several kinds of canvas used in fancy work.

WORSTED CANVAS worked in cross-stitch in the different colors of fancy silks, or crewels, makes very pretty tidies, table covers, bureau covers, etc. It comes in all the shades of red, blue, buff,

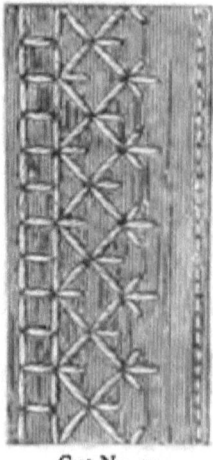
Cut No. 29.

Cut No. 30.

and in black and white, while the width is the same as in most other canvases, viz.: half yard, three-fourths yard, one yard, and one yard and a half.

JAVA CANVAS comes in linen and cotton, and the worsted canvas mentioned before belongs to this style of canvas. It comes in almost all shades, and is put to almost all uses.

MUMMY CANVAS is in appearance much like the mummy cloth, it is woven in irregular meshes, and is the natural linen color. It may be worked in crewel zephyr, or silk, and is used for chair seats, or cushions, sofa pillows, etc., etc. There are a variety of fancy canvases more or less used, but these given are the standard.

In cloth fabrics there is also a large variety which are used in the various kinds of fancy work. These include felt, mummy cloth, broadcloth, and Canton flannel, which now comes in all the fashionable shades of olive, old gold, maroon, blue, pink, etc., and is much used for table covers, lambrequins, portierres, etc.

For finer work there is plush, sateen, and satin, and in fact at present almost anything is applied for draperies and fancy decoration.

In working material, CREWEL has been heretofore mentioned, and takes the lead. It is a soft, glossy, slightly wiry wool, and works as easily as silk. It can be bought in any shade, and is sold in skeins, or by weight.

The GERMANTOWN and BERLIN WOOLS are very like in texture and chiefly used in knitting or crotcheting shawls, or house sacks, and embroidering rugs.

SAXONY YARN is much used in crocheting lace for the bottom of flannel skirts, or flannel house sacks, and comes in all shades.

The silks used mostly are embroidery silk and filloselle, although the old-fashioned saddler's silk is sometimes found useful in making fringes, and also in chain stitching. Filloselle is an untwisted coarse silk, and is composed of a number of threads very slightly twisted. it is very pretty for touching up the strong lights in crewel embroidery and is used altogether by many in embroidering small designs on satin or plush, as it shades very prettily, and when the work is finished, if done neatly, has the appearance of satin.

CHENILLE, or ARRASENE, is now much used in embroidery. It must always be cut in short lengths, as it wears off, after repeatedly being drawn through the work, particularly if the fabric is fine.

BEADS in all colors have been introduced into fancy work, and can be purchased in colors to shade the same as in crewel or silk.

GOLD and SILVER threads are used for outlining embroidery. They are quite effective when used judiciously, but are not advisable as they very soon tarnish and the work loses its beauty to the eye when outlined by a tarnished cord.

It is impossible in a book of this size to give directions for making any variety of articles, and yet, perhaps, a few hints or suggestions thrown out, might aid those who are too remote from the city or large towns, to receive suggestions from the variety of articles usually displayed for sale in the stores or shops.

We have seen a very pretty table cover made of maroon felt, with a pattern in crewel embroidery of daisies, ferns and wheat, worked in the corners. The edge of the cover was finished with a fringe of the prevailing color.

Pretty table covers may be made of the basket flannel now so much in style, with a border in some simple, pretty design, with a fringe of crewel tied in around the edge.

A table scarf can be made of any desirable color of felt or sateen; for the center, have the scarf about one and a half yards long, with a four-inch band of plush of the same or a contrasting color upon the ends. Finish the ends with fringe, or crewel tassels, alternating with small silk balls of different colors. A spray of flowers in embroidery can be worked just above the band of plush if desired. Applique fans, placed just above the border also make a very pretty decoration, or a spray of golden rod worked in plush stitch.

Pretty table scarfs may be made of felt by embroidering a spray of wild roses, or some other simple flower in one corner, and then tying in a fringe of crewel, or the same may be finished, by cutting out the ends in vandykes or points, and hanging upon and between each point a tassel made of the felt. To make these tassels, take a piece of felt, three or four inches in width, according to the length of tassel desired, and seven or eight inches long; cut the felt in narrow strips, say an eighth of an inch in width, to within a half inch of the entire width, when this is done roll tightly up and fasten, and your tassel is made, the uncut part answering for the top of the tassel. Embroider this top a little with some bright colored silk in fancy stitches, drawing a thread of twisted silk through the top, with which to fasten it to the material, and you thus have a handsome and very inexpensive tassel.

Very pretty mantel lambrequins are made of plain plush of some desirable color, with a spray of wild flowers, golden rod in plush stitch, and daisies, or thistles and buttercups, wild roses, etc., etc., worked upon either end. The ends are cut a little deeper than the remainder of the lambrequin and cut square. Then finished with plush tassels set on about two inches apart, or bordered with a fringe, this makes a lambrequin handsome enough for any parlor. Mantel valances are simple straight bands from ten to twelve inches in width, and can be made of felt, plush, satin, or in fact almost any fabric to match the room where they are to be placed. They should be edged with fringe or small tassels.

Valances for windows are made to match, and are quite inexpensive and very neat, made of felt with a plush of contrasting color used as a border, with fancy stitches placed above the border in embroidery silk. The window valances should be from fifteen to eighteen inches in width according to the height of the room. Some ladies who use the brush in painting, make valances and table scarfs of a material upon which they can use color, or else use a satin border, and upon that paint some pretty design. In all these home decorations much depends upon the taste of the individual, so many pretty things suggest themselves if one has taste and a knowledge of needlework in its various forms.

KNITTING.

This branch of woman's education has in the past few years been much neglected; the time was, when our grandmothers would have considered a young lady's education incomplete until she was able at least to knit her own stockings. Knitting machines have done away largely with the necessity of that kind of work, and yet the importance of knitting can hardly be overestimated, as a machine can never reach the perfection of hand-knit articles. Supposing that our readers have all learned the stitch, we will give only the terms used in knitting. The first term used is to *cast on*, which is done by making a loop and placing it on the needle which is held in the left hand; when with the right hand needle you knit it off without removing the needle out of the first stitch. Having done this pass the second stitch on the needle and so continue until the required number is CAST ON.

When a piece of work is completed, knit two stitches with the left hand and pull the first over the second, knit another stitch and pull the first over the second, and repeat this until only one stitch remains, when you are to pull your thread through this and fasten it securely; this is called CASTING OFF.

TO INCREASE a stitch, take one loop over the needle, and proceed as before, and it will be found that on the following row, by knitting this loop, a stitch will have been gained and an open stitch left in the knitting.

TO DECREASE a stitch, knit two stitches together; this is called narrowing.

TO SEAM OR PURL, the right hand needle is slipped in the loop in front of the left one, and the thread after passing between the two is brought round it; it is then worked as before. The thread is always brought forward before beginning a purled stitch.

TO SLIP A STITCH, is merely to pass a stitch from the left hand needle to right hand needle without knitting it.

We give below directions for edgings and many other useful articles.

KNITTED LACE

For edging flannel skirts, sacks, etc., knit of Saxony yarn.

Take up fourteen stitches, knit across once plain, slip off the first stitch without knitting, knit four, narrow the rest of the stitches, putting thread over twice each time. There will be one stitch left, knit that, putting thread over twice. Knit back plain, and you will have five holes caused by the loops formed by putting thread over twice. Then slip off one, knit five, narrow and knit back plain as before. Next time knit six plain, and so on until you have made five holes six times, that is, until you have six rows of five holes. Then knit across twice plain, *a* slip and bind once, narrow five times, putting thread over twice, knit the rest of the stitches plain *b*. Repeat from *a* to *b* till only fourteen stitches are left on the needle. This finishes one scallop.

NARROW EDGE.

Cast on eight stitches; knit across plain.

1. Slip one, knit one, thread over twice, seam two together, knit two, thread over twice, knit one, thread over once, knit one.

2. Knit four, purl one, knit two, thread over twice, seam two together, knit two.

3. Slip one, knit one, thread over twice, seam two together, the rest plain.

4. Bind off three, knit three, thread over twice, seam two together, knit two.

Begin again.

NARROW EDGING.

Cast on eleven stitches.

1. Knit three, make one, narrow one, knit one, make one, narrow one, make two, narrow one, knit one.

2. Knit three, seam one, put back thread, knit two, make one, narrow one, knit one, make one, narrow one, knit one.

3. Knit three, make one, narrow one, knit one, make one, narrow one, knit four.

4. Knit two, slip and bind, knit four, make one, narrow one, make one, narrow one, knit one.

LEAF EDGING.

Cast on twenty-six stitches; knit back plain.

1. Knit two, over, narrow, knit one, over, knit two, slip one, narrow, throw slipped stitch over, knit two, over, knit one, over, and knit two, slip one, narrow, throw slipped stitch over, knit two, over, knit two, over, narrow, over twice, knit two. There are now twenty-eight stitches.

2. Knit three, purl one, knit one, over, narrow, purl seventeen, knit one, over, narrow, knit one.

3. Knit two, over, narrow, knit two, over, knit one, slip one, narrow, throw slipped stitch over, knit one, over, knit three, over, knit one, slip one, narrow, slip stitch over, knit one, over, knit three, over, narrow, knit four. There are twenty-eight stitches.

4. Knit five, over, narrow, purl seventeen, knit one, over, narrow, knit one.

5. Knit two, over, narrow, knit three, over, slip one, narrow, throw slipped stitch over, over, knit five, over, slip one, narrow, throw slipped one over, over, knit four, over, narrow, over twice, narrow, over twice, knit two.

6. Knit three, purl one, knit two, purl one, knit one, over, narrow, purl seventeen, knit one, over, narrow, knit one. Thirty-one stitches.

7. Knit two, over, narrow, narrow, knit two, over, knit one, over, knit two, slip one, narrow, throw slipped stitch over, knit two, over, knit one, over, knit two, slip one, knit one, slip stitch over, knit one, over, narrow, knit seven.

8. Knit eight, over, narrow, purl seventeen, knit one, over, narrow, knit one.

9. Knit two, over, narrow, narrow, knit one, over, knit three, over, knit one, slip one, narrow, slipped stitch over, knit one, over, knit three, over, knit one, slip one, knit one, slipped stitch over, knit one, over, narrow, over twice, narrow, over twice, narrow, over twice, narrow, knit one. Thirty-four stitches remain.

10. Knit three, purl one, knit two, purl one, knit two, purl one,

knit one, over, narrow, purl seventeen, knit one, over, narrow, knit one.

11. Knit two, over, narrow, narrow, over, knit five, over, slip one, narrow, slip stitch over, over, knit five, over, slip one, knit one, slip stitch over, knit one, over, narrow, knit ten.

12. Cast off eight stitches, knit two, over, narrow, purl seventeen, knit one, over, narrow, knit one. This finishes one scallop.

SOLID POINT LACE.

· Cast on sixteen stitches.

1. Knit three plain, thread over twice, purl two together, knit two, thread over twice, narrow, thread over twice, narrow, knit five.

2. Knit seven, purl one, knit two, purl one, knit two, thread over twice, purl two together, knit three.

3. Knit three, thread over twice, purl two together, knit thirteen.

4. Knit thirteen, thread over twice, purl two together, knit three.

5. Knit three, thread over twice, purl two together, knit two, thread over twice, narrow, thread over twice, narrow, thread over twice, narrow, knit five.

6. Knit seven, purl one, knit two, purl one, knit two, purl one, knit two, thread over twice, purl two together, knit three.

7. Knit three, thread over twice, purl two together, knit sixteen.

8. Bind off five stitches, or till you have sixteen stitches on both needles, knit ten, thread over twice, purl two together, knit three.

Commence at first row.

KNITTING PATTERN FOR VARIOUS PURPOSES.

This pattern is suitable for making many useful little articles. It is pretty for babies' blankets or cot covers lined with silk, or knitted in very coarse wool for traveling rugs. Different kinds of wool must, of course, be selected, according to purpose for which the knitting is intended.

Cast on any number of stitches that will divide by four, and allow besides one for each end.

1. Slip one, *make one, slip one, knit three, draw the slipped stitch over the three knitted ones, repeat from *, knit one.
2. Knit one, purl all but last stitch, which knit plain.
3. Same as first row.
4. Same as second row.

Repeat the first and second rows alternately, till of the desired length.

To make a stitch, simply bring the wool forward as for seaming.

CHILD'S KNITTED COLLAR.

Use forty, fifty, or sixty cotton, with corresponding needles. Cast on twenty-eight stitches.

1. Knit three, narrow, knit two, over, knit one, over, narrow, over, narrow, over, knit two, narrow, knit four, narrow, knit two, over, knit one, over, narrow, over, knit one.

The second, fourth, and other even rows are purled.

3. Knit two, narrow, knit two, over, knit three, over, narrow, over, narrow, over, knit two, narrow, knit two, narrow, knit two, over, knit three, over, narrow, over, knit one.
5. Knit one, narrow, knit two, over, knit five, over, narrow, over, narrow, over, knit two, narrow twice, knit two, over, knit five, over, narrow, over, knit one.
7. Knit six, narrow, knit two, over, narrow, over, knit one, over, knit one, over, knit two, narrow, knit two, narrow, knit one, narrow, knit two, over, narrow, over, narrow.
9. Knit five, narrow, knit two, over, narrow, over, narrow, over, knit three, over, knit two, narrow, knit two, narrow, knit two, over, narrow, over, narrow.
11. Knit four, narrow, knit two, over, narrow, over, narrow, over, knit five, over, knit two, narrow twice, knit two, over, narrow, over, narrow.

KNITTED SKIRT.

The color can be red, drab, white or blue. Five skeins of Germantown wool is required, and large needles, (same as for Afghan.) Cast on one hundred and nine stitches.

1. Seam across.
2. Knit plain.

Scallop now begins. Slip first stitch, put worsted over, knit four plain, slip one, narrow one and bind, knit four plain, put worsted over, knit one, put worsted over, knit four, slip one, narrow one and bind, knit four plain, etc. At the end of needle seam back, when you have made five slips and binds in one scallop, knit plain one row, seam next row, then plain one row, then begin scallop as before.

KNITTED SILK MITTENS.

Here is a simple pattern, knit with two steel needles (the very finest) and two balls of knitting silk.

Cast on eighty stitches, knit plain both ways, forming a rib with each back and forth.

* Knit twenty ribs, widening at the top of the needle each rib except last two. Knit twenty ribs, narrowing at the top of the needle each rib except first two. Knit three ribs plain. Repeat from *. Bind off.

For the thumb cast on twenty-two stitches.

* Knit seven ribs, widening at the top and bottom of the needle for each rib. Knit seven ribs, narrowing at the top and widening at the bottom of the needle for each rib. Knit one rib plain. Repeat from *, only narrowing instead of widening at bottom of needle. Bind off all but three at bottom of needle for thumb gusset. Knit six ribs, widening at top of the needle for each rib. Knit six ribs, narrowing at the top of the needle for each rib. Bind off. Sew together.

This makes a loose wrist. If a tight wrist is wished cast on only sixty stitches in the beginning and when the mitten is sewed together, take up the stitches of the wrist on four needles, knitting two plain and one purl, alternately for as many rounds as desired.

KNITTED GLOVES.

Cast on eighteen stitches on two needles, and nineteen on the third needle.

1. Knit one, put the yarn back, take off one stitch, knit one, put

the yarn back, take off one and knit the next one, and so on all round.

2. Put the yarn back, take off the single stitch, knit the stitch and loop as one stitch, and so on all round (putting the yarn back and taking off the single stitch and knitting the double stitch every time) until you have knit it four inches and a half long, then take off fifteen stitches on to a thread for the thumb, cast on fifteen stitches on a needle to take the place of those taken off, and then knit round as before until you have knit two and one-fourth inches, then drop off thirteen stitches on a thread for the little finger, then cast on three stitches on a needle to take the place of those taken off, then knit round four times the same as before. For the next finger drop off on to a thread seventeen stitches, then cast on five stitches to take the place of those taken off, knit round once, then take off on to a thread nineteen stitches for the middle finger, and cast six stitches to take the place of those taken off, then knit till the finger is long enough, and then narrow off as you would a stocking.

SHELL FOR KNITTED COUNTERPANE.

With No. 8 Dexter cotton and medium-sized steel needles cast on 44 stitches. Knit 1st, 3d and 5th rows plain. 2d row: Knit 2 together, over; repeat this 21 times, then knit 2 together.

4th row: Knit 2 together and over, 21 times, knit 1.
6th row: Slip 1, knit 2, narrow, knit the rest plain.
7th row: Slip 1, knit 2, narrow, purl all but 4, knit these plain.

The 8th, 9th, 11th, 12th, 14th, 15th, 17th, 18th, 20th, 21st, 23d, 24th, 26th, 27th, 29th, 30th, 32d, 33d, 35th, 36th, 38th, 39th, 40th, 41st, and 42d rows are all knit like the 6th row.

The 10th, 13th, 16th, 19th, 22d, 25th, 28th, 31st, 34th and 37th rows are all knit like the 7th row.

43d row: Slip 1, knit 2, narrow, knit 2.
44th row: Slip 1, knit 1, narrow, knit 1.
45th row: Slip 1, narrow, knit 1.
46th row: Slip 1, narrow, slip the first stitch over the last and draw the thread through.

In joining these shells place each narrowed point to the center of the first row of another shell, and allow all the points to run downward, then one can easily see where the other shells join in, and sew together.

INFANT'S KNITTED SHIRT.

One skein of cream white Shetland wool. Two quite fine bone needles. The following are the directions for one-half of the garment, which is joined under the arms:

1. Cast on 82 stitches.
2. Purl across.
3. Knit across plain.
4. Slip off first stitch, narrow 1, 2 plain, thread over and knit 1, thread over and knit 2, narrow 2, knit 2, thread over and knit 1, thread over and knit 2, narrow 2, knit 2, etc., across.
5. Purl across.
6. Same as 4.
7. Knit across plain.
8. Purl across.
9. Knit across plain.
10. Begin at 4 and so on to 10 until you have four times knitted the inclusive rows, and you will have four rows of scallops, which form the bottom of the shirt.

Then knit 2 plain, purl 2, 2 plain, purl 2, and so across. Make 45 rows in this manner, being careful to have them match, so as to give the work the appearance of seaming.

Cast on 16 stitches for the shoulder. Then knit across the entire width, shoulder and body. Purl across. Knit 2, thread over and knit 1, narrow 1, knit 2, etc., across. This last row makes a row of holes, through which narrow ribbon can be drawn to make the neck smaller, if desired. Bind off.

The sleeve is made of the four rows of scalloping in the same way as that round the bottom of the body, and joined to the shoulder.

INFANT'S SOCKS.

It takes about two bunches of zephyr worsted, say one of white and one of blue.

Cast on forty-seven stitches, knit back and forth until you have four rows, put on the other color, knit back and forth plain, then knit two together, narrow, two together, narrow, two together, to end of needle, knit back plain. Take the other color, knit plain until you have three rows, again take the other color, knit two together, narrow, same as before, for rows of holes for strings. Then knit plain again until you have five rows of plain.

Cast off on a string seventeen stitches, knit thirteen, cast off on string seventeen, knit the thirteen plain, back and forth, until you have fifteen rows on right side.

Take up stitches on left hand first, same as heel of a stocking, which will be fifteen, same number as rows, then knit the seventeen you cast off on string. Knit round to the other side, take up same as before, put on the other color for foot. Knit round back and forth until you have ten rows on right side, narrow on each end until you have thirteen rows, then knit in middle, double together and bind off.

These socks are finished with a crocheted scallop at the top and a cord run through the lower row of holes. Finish each end of cord with pretty tassels.

KNITTED TIDY.

With No. 10 cotton cast on 31 stitches, 1st row: knit 15, narrow, knit thirteen, make 1, knit 1. 2d row, purl 15, purl 2 together, purl 13, make 1, purl 1. 3d row same as 1st: 4th row same as 2d; 5th row same as 1st; 6th row same as 1st; 7th row same as 2d, etc., reversing the 6th row so that it will come in ribs. The strips may be knit any length desired according to the size you want your tidy; also you can vary the number of strips. Sew or crochet the strips together and finish with a fringe at both ends.

BABY'S COUVRETTE.

This pattern makes a series of holes, and is pretty knitted in white with narrow blue or pink ribbon run through the holes, and with bows at the corners.

Cast on any number of stitches which can be divided by seven.

1st row: Thread forward, slip 1, knit 1, pass the slipped stitch over the knitted one, knit 5.

2d row: Purl.

3d row: Thread forward, slip 1, knit 1, pass slipped stitch over, knit 1, purl 3, knit 1.

4th row: Purl 1, knit 1, thread forward, knit 2 together, purl 3.

5th row: Thread forward, slip 1, knit 1, pass slipped stitch over, knit 1, purl 3, knit 1.

6th row: Purl.

7th row: Thread forward, slip 1, knit 1, pass slipped stitch over, knit 5.

8th row: Purl.

Begin again at 3d row.

KNITTED UNDER-DRAWERS.

The material is four-thread fleecy wool or yarn of equivalent quality. A pair of No. 4 needles and some No. 8 needles are required. The wool may be either scarlet, white or chinchilla. With No. 8 needles cast on 200 stitches for the body and 1 extra. This one extra stitch is to be marked by a colored thread in the middle of the work to form a center to the body. 1st row: knit plain 100 stitches, purl 1 (the center stitch), knit plain 100. 2d row: knit 2, purl 2, repeat to end of row. 3d row: knit 2, purl 2, repeat to end of row. Then repeat the last row 3 times more. In the 7th row increase a stitch (by putting wool over the needle) on each side the center stitch. All the rest of the row is knit 2, purl 2. 8th row: like 2d row. 9th, 10th and 11th rows the same. 12th row: like 7th row. Next 4 rows like 2d row. 17th row: like 7th row. Go on in this manner, increasing a stitch on each side the center stitch in every fifth row, until you have worked 68 rows. Then divide the stitches in half for the legs. Knit on the first half of the stitches 16 plain rows, still keeping the rib of 2 plain and 2 purl. Now, at the 17th row, with four needles, join the work and knit 11 rounds, 2 plain, 2 purl. Twelfth round: decrease 1 (that is, knit 2 together) on each side of the seam stitch, which now is the stitch where the work is joined.* Thirteenth, 14th and 15th rounds, ribbed by knitting 2 plain, 2 purl, as above. Sixteenth round: decrease 1 on each side the seam stitch again. Repeat from *, knitting 4 ribbed rounds as above between each round of decreasing. Work in this manner until you have only 54 stitches left on the needles. Now knit 20 rows of knit 1, purl 1, and cast off loosely. Now take up the stitches on the other leg, and repeat the above directions exactly. When both legs are finished take up the center stitch of the body and knit a gusset. This is done thus: Knit 1, turn, take up the stitch on the last row of leg, knit it, turn, slip the first stitch, knit the next, knit the first stitch on the other leg, turn, slip 1, knit 2, increase, knit one on the next leg, turn, slip 1, knit 4. Take up one on the next leg, turn, slip one, knit all the rest and take one up at the end of each row until the stitches are all knitted up to the join of the legs. Then continue to knit, decreasing one at the end of each row as you take up the stitches on the other side of the leg, and up the front of the body, until you have only one stitch left; knit this, take up the stitches on the sides of the two fronts, and knit three rows. Sew over strongly in the front. Then take a crochet needle and crochet a band of ten rows for the waist.

KNITTED MITTENS.

With common sized yarn cast on sixty stitches, twenty on each of three needles, and knit with the fourth.

1. Knit around plain.

2. Knit six, purl one, then knit seven in this way, viz.: knit one, thread over and knit one, thread over and knit one, until seven are knitted, purl one. Continue this from the beginning with the three needles, and the work will come out even, and end by purling one.

3. Knit six, purl one, slip one, knit one, pass the slipped stitch over the knitted one, knit plain to last loop and stitch, which narrow, purl one, and so on with this round, ending with purl one.

4. Knit this and succeeding rounds same as the third, until the open-work stripe is narrowed down to seven, then commence again with second round, and knit through the whole until the open-work stripe is narrowed down to seven the second time.

Now, instead of knitting the six plain, slip off the first three on to a fifth needle, knit last three, then knit the three on the fifth needle, knitting the third stitch last. As will be seen, this twists the first half of the stripe over the last; in every other way this round is same as second, twisting every plain six stitches, and work the whole down to the original seven the second time as before, then twist again, for which use the fifth needle must be kept handy.

Knit in this way until the wrist is two or three inches long, ending with a twist round, and of course there will be seven in the open-work stripe. Carry one purl, twist row, one purl, the over and knit one row, the one purl, twist row, and one purl, up the back, until long enough to narrow off; knitting remainder of mitten and thumb plain, and the very same way our mothers and grandmothers always did. The mitten fits nicely by narrowing occasionally inside of the hand, commencing one and one-half inches perhaps beyond the thumb gore.

If an extra sized mitten is needed, or fine Saxony yarn is used, cast on sixty-eight stitches, and purl two every time instead of one.

Be careful and not make both mittens for one hand. A small bow and ends of narrow ribbon, same shade or some darker than the mittens, placed at the back, where the wrists and hands join, improve the looks.

I have seen wristers knit this way that were very pretty.

One can twist at every third seven, instead of the second, as given, especially with fine yarn.

FLY FRINGE.

For tidies, shawls, mats and other articles, whether knitted or crocheted, a simple and common edging, known in the shops as " fly fringe," may be made as follows:

When several yards of it are required take two studs or nails on opposite sides of a room or as far apart as may be desired. With the cotton or wool to be used, fasten to one of the studs and wind the material around the two studs half a dozen times, or more if a heavy fly is wanted.

Now take the ball and tie tightly round the loose strands, as they may be called, of this long rope, just below the first stud or nail. Make another tie three-quarters of an inch or an inch lower, not cutting off the thread, but making a tight double hitch. Repeat these double hitches at the same intervals till the second stud is reached.

Next take a pair of scissors and between each tie cut the threads through, all except the one which was used to make the ties. This remains intact from the beginning to the end. The other threads, when severed, form little tufts, bound together by the ties at regular intervals, very much like the insertions in the tail of a boy's kite. The tufts, or flies, can be made larger or smaller by increasing or diminishing the number of threads wound around the studs, and can be placed any distance apart by regulating the double hitches or ties. The fringe can obviously be made of any particular color, or mixture of colors.

BRIOCHE.

A pretty style of knitting is known as the Brioche stitch. It is also easy and rapid, and is popular with knitters for a wide range of articles. Here is a comforter for a little boy or girl, which will be a fair example of what it is like.

With two wooden needles, No. 8 to No. 6, and single zephyr wool, of any desired color, cast on seventy stitches. Knit two plain stitches; then * make one, slip one, knit two together; repeat from * till only two stitches are left; these are to be knit plain. The first two and last two stitches are to be knit plain throughout, and are meant for an edging. The brioche stitch, as will be seen, works in threes. The slip stitch is always to be taken off as in purling. After the first row the stitch to be slipped separates itself from the rest, and the two to be knit as one fall naturally together, so that there is no difficulty in knowing when to slip and when to knit. Remember not to "make one" before the last two edge stitches, as the habit of doing so after knitting two together is almost sure to lead a careless knitter into this mistake. Every row is the same as the first. Continue knitting till the comforter is a yard to a yard and a half long; then cast off loosely. A knitted fringe can be added to each end if desired.

LADY'S SLEEVELESS JACKET.

For a soft, light jacket, 3 fold Berlin wool may be used with No. 14 or No. 13 needles. The size of this pattern, as that of many others, may be greatly modified by changing the size of the needles, and using finer or coarser wool to correspond with them.

The jacket is knitted in brioche stitch, which has already been fully explained. Front and back are knitted separately, and joined with fine sewing. The border, knitted after the directions given, is sewn on separately. Begin the back with 203 stitches. The 3 stitches are worked *plain each row* in the middle of the back.—1st row. * Wool forward, slip 1, knit 1, repeat from * 49 more times. Knit 3, repeat from the first * 50 times.—2nd row. * Wool forward, slip 1, knit 2 together, the two lying over each other, repeat 49 more times, knit 3, repeat from the last * 50 times ; knit 2 more rows like the 2nd row.—In the 5th row you begin the decreasings for the hips. Decrease after the first 2 ribs of brioche, and before the two last ; decrease by knitting the slip stitch of the 3rd rib *with* the two together of the 2nd rib, and the double stitch with the slip one of the 4th rib. You also decrease after and before the 16 stitches or 8 ribs on each side the middle 3 in the same manner.— 6th, 7th and 8th rows. Plain Brioche without decreasing.—9th row. Decrease on each side the middle again, 7 ribs from the middle—3 rows plain.—13th row. Decrease on the 6th rib on each side the waist, and also before and after the two first and last ribs.—3 rows brioche.—17th row. Decrease in the middle only, as in the 9th row, but on the 5th rib.—3 rows brioche.—21st row. Decrease in the 4 places.—3 rows brioche.—25th row. Decrease in the waist only.—3 rows brioche.—29th row. Decrease 4 times, as in the 21st row.—3 rows brioche.—33d row. Knit the same number of ribs before and after the middle, and decrease another rib on each side of it —3 rows brioche.—37th row. Decrease in all 4 places.—41st row. Like the 33rd row.—3 rows plain.—45th row. Like the 33rd row.—3 rows plain.— * 49th row. Decrease at the ends only.—3 rows plain. Repeat from * twice more. This brings you to the waist. * You now increase a rib from the side piece of the back every 4th row, making it one stripe further from the middle on each side; you increase by bringing wool forward and taking up the stitch between the last on the needles. Knit 3 more rows, then increase on each side and in the back ; repeat from * until you have 6 increasings on each side, which brings you to the armhole. Cast off loosely on each side 10 stitches or 5 ribs, knit 64 rows brioche, keeping the seam in the middle. You now decrease for the shoulders ; this do on each side a whole rib at the beginning of every row. Decrease until there are only 60 on the needle, and cast them off loosely. Plain rows mean, of course, plain brioche rows.

The fronts are knitted alike; one is given. As the brioche knitting is the same on both sides, it can be turned and no alteration is needed in the decreasings. Cast on 108 stitches, knit the two first rows in the manner described for the back, and in the 5th row decrease after the 2d rib under the *arm* only. The other edge is kept plain. Decrease after every 6th row of plain brioche, and knit 60 rows. Then knit for the piece under the arm; knit 45 rows, increasing every 7th row on the one side, for the waist. You next knit 60 rows. Decrease for the arm by casting off 10 stitches; knit 64 rows, casting off or decreasing one stitch every other row on the same side, until you have the 64 rows. You now decrease for the shoulder in the same manner as the back; after the 18th row decrease for the neck by casting off 8, after this by knitting 2 together every row in beginning the row. Sew the shoulders and jacket together. The border is very handsome, knit in gold silk, and laid over the edge; the pattern is given below. The neck and armholes are finished by knitting 2 rows of DC. (double crochet), then a row of * 4 Ch., 1 DC. on the next DC.; repeat from *.

For the border cast on 23 stitches, and knit back.—1st row. Slip 1, knit 1, make 1, knit 2, knit 2 together, purl 1, knit 2 together, knit 2, purl 1, knit 2, knit 2 together, purl 1, knit 2 together, knit 2, make 1, knit 2.—2nd row. Slip 1, knit 1, purl 4, knit 1, purl 3, knit 1, purl 3, knit 1, purl 4, knit 2.—3rd row. Slip 1, knit 1, make 1, knit 1, make 1, knit 1, knit 2 together, purl 1, knit 2 together, knit 1, purl 1, knit 1, knit 2 together, purl 1, knit 2 together, knit 1, make 1, knit 1, make 1, knit 2.—4th row. Slip 1, knit 1, purl 5, knit 1, purl 2, knit 1, purl 2, knit 1, purl 5, knit 2.—5th row. Slip 1, knit 1, make 1, knit 3, make 1, knit 2 together, purl 1, knit 2 together, purl 1, knit 2 together, purl 1, knit 2 together, make 1, knit 3, make 1, knit 2.—6th row. Slip 1, knit 1, purl 6, knit 1, purl 1, knit 1, purl 1, knit 1, purl 6, knit 2.—7th row. Slip 1, knit 1, make 1, knit 5, make 1, knit 3 together, purl 1, knit 3 together, make 1, knit 5, make 1, knit 2.—8th row. Slip 1, knit 1, purl 8, knit 1, purl 8, knit 2.—9th row. Slip 1, knit 1, make 1, knit 7, make 1, knit 3 together, make 1, knit 7, make 1, knit 2.—10th row. Slip 1, knit 1, purl 19, knit 2, repeat from the 1st row.

KNITTED LACE COLLARS.

With cotton No. 40 and needles No. 24 cast on fifteen stitches. First row: Knit 2, make 1, knit 1, make 1, knit 2, slip 1, knit two together and pass the slipped stitch over; knit 2, make 1, knit 1, make 1, knit two, slip 1, knit 1 and pass the slipped stitch over.

Second row and every alternate row, purl all but 2 and knit them plain.

Third row: Knit 2, make 1, knit 3, make 1, knit 1, slip 1, knit 2 together and pass the slipped stitch over; knit 1, make 1, knit 3, make 1, knit 1, slip 1, knit 1, and pass the slipped stitch over.

Fifth row: Knit 2, make 1, knit 5, make 1, slip 1, knit 2 together and pass the slipped stitch over; make 1, knit 5, make 1, slip 1, knit 1 and pass the slipped stitch over.

Seventh row: Knit 4, slip 1, knit 2 together and pass the slipped stitch over; knit 2, make 1, knit 1, make 1, knit 2, slip 1, knit 2 together and pass the slipped stitch over; knit 2, make 1, knit 1.

Ninth row: Knit 3, slip 1, knit 2 together and pass the slipped stitch over; knit 1, make 1, knit 3, make 1, knit 1, slip 1, knit 2 together and pass the slipped stitch over; knit 1, make 1, knit 2.

Eleventh row: Knit 2, slip 1, knit 2 together and pass the slipped stitch over; make 1, knit 5, make 1, slip 1, knit 2 together and pass the slipped stitch over; make 1, knit 3.

Twelfth row: As second. Repeat these 12 rows until the work is long enough. Pick up the stitches at the neck and knit one row, taking two together every ten stitches. Knit a few more rows and cast off. Now trim it with the following edging:

With the same materials and needles cast on 16 stitches and knit back plain. Then—

First row: Knit 2, * make 1, knit 2 together, repeat from * once; knit 2, * make 1, knit 2 together, repeat from * twice; make 1, knit 2.

Second row: Purl 11, knit 6.

Third row: Knit 2, * make 1, knit 2 together, repeat from * once; knit 3, * make 1, knit two together, repeat from * twice; make 1, knit 2.

Fourth row: Purl 12, knit 6.

Fifth row: Knit 2, * make 1, knit 2 together, repeat from * once;

knit 2, make 1, knit 2, * make 1, knit 2 together, repeat from * twice; make 1, knit 2.

Sixth row: Purl 14, knit 6.

Seventh row: Knit 2, * make 1, knit 2 together, repeat from * once; knit 2 together, make 1, knit 1, make 1, knit 2 together, knit 1, * make 1, knit 2 together, repeat from * twice; make 1, knit 2.

Eighth row: Purl 15, knit 6.

Ninth row: Knit 2, * make 1, knit 2 together, repeat from * once; knit 1, make 1, knit 3, make 1, knit 2 together, knit 1, * make 1, knit 2 together, repeat from * twice; make 1, knit 2.

Tenth row: Purl 16, knit 6.

Eleventh row: Knit 2, * knit 1, knit 2 together, repeat from * once; knit 1, make 1, knit 2 together, knit 1, knit 2 together, make 1, knit 2 together, knit 9.

Twelfth row: Knit 1, * knit 2 together, make 1, repeat from * three times; purl 7, knit 6.

Thirteenth row: Knit 2, * make 1, knit 2 together, repeat from * once; knit 2, make 1, knit 3 together, make 1, knit 11.

Fourteenth row: Knit 1, knit 2 together, * make 1, knit 2 together, repeat from * three times; purl 5, knit 6.

Fifteenth row: Knit 2, * make 1, knit 2 together, repeat from * once; knit 1, knit 2 together, make 1, knit 2 together, knit 10.

Sixteenth row: Knit 1, knit 2 together, * make 1, knit 2 together, repeat from * three times; purl 3, knit 6.

Seventeenth row: Knit 2, * make 1, knit 2 together, repeat from * once; knit 13.

Eighteenth row: Like 16th, but purl 2.

Nineteenth row: Knit 2, * make 1, knit 2 together, repeat from * once; knit 2 together, knit 10.

Twentieth row: Like 16th, without purling any.

Twenty-first row: Knit 2, * make 1, knit 2 together, repeat from * once; knit 10.

Twenty-second row: Plain knitting.

Repeat from the beginning as often as may be desired, and then sew the edging to the piece first worked. It will be seen that the work of the collar consists of three parts—first, the open work body; second, the narrow plain band on the neck or inner side, so knit as to curve the collar; third, the edging to be sewn on the body.

The edging above described is well suited, when worked in proper materials, for the trimming of a counterpane or any large piece of work

INFANT'S SHIRT.

Cast on 73 stitches. It should be understood that when stitches are set up they must be knitted once across plain and very loose in order to make a good edge, and first stitches are always slipped without knitting for the same reason.

1st row: Slip 1st, slip 2d, knit one plain and bind (or cast) 2d over it, over, 1 plain, over, 1 plain, over, 1 plain, over, 1 plain, over, 1 plain, over, 1 plain, over, 1 plain, narrow (or knit 2 together), purl 1; repeat from " slip 2d " to the end of the row.

2d row: Slip 1st, purl 16, knit 1 plain, purl 16, knit 1 plain; repeat to end of row.

3d row: Slip 1st, slip 2d, knit 3d plain and bind 2d over it, knit 12 plain, narrow, purl 1; repeat from " slip 2d " to end of row.

4th row: Slip 1st, purl 14, knit 1 plain, purl 14, knit 1 plain; repeat to end of row.

5th row: Slip 1st, slip 2d, knit 3d plain and bind 2d over 3d, knit 10 plain, narrow, purl 1, and repeat as in 3d and 1st rows to the end.

6th row: Slip 1st, purl 10, purl 2 together, knit 1 plain, purl 10, purl 2 together, knit 1 plain, and repeat to the end of row.

This makes the whole pattern, and when done should leave the 73 stitches begun with. It is to be repeated six times, which makes the bottom part of the shirt body. Above this it should be simply ribbed by knitting 2 plain and 2 purl, 2 plain and 2 purl back and forth till it is as long as desired; 9 inches is about right. Then knit a row of holes across the top for the cord which draws the neck, and cast off. Seventy stitches are enough for the ribbed part, and the three extra stitches may be disposed of by binding them off gradually, anywhere throughout the 1st row of the ribbed part. They must not be done all together or it would show. Two pieces knit like the above, and sewed together with the wool (which should be 3-threaded Saxony yarn), make the body, and these side seams are to be left open 4½ inches from the top, for the sleeve. Any pretty lace pattern of 13 to 15 stitches will answer for this. Having made 12 points knit about 14 or 15 rows plain, which will make a little square piece on the end. This is for a gusset and is to be sewed to the other end like any gusset cut on a chemise sleeve. Then sew it into the place left in the side seam with the point set in where the seam was left open.

The holes round the top of the body are made in this way, beginning on the right side, of course: Slip 1, over, narrow, 1 plain, over, narrow, 1 plain, over, to end of row. Knit back all plain, then cast off.

If they are required to be high in the neck it can be done by narrowing off gradually (at what would be the top otherwise) to fit the shoulder; probably eight stitches on each side would be enough. An open place must be left in one breadth for the neck. This is easily done by dividing the number of stitches by 2, and knitting the two halves up separately. This leaves the little slit for the front.

KNITTED JACKET FOR INFANTS.

The wool for this pretty jacket may be either white Shetland or white single zephyr; it depends upon whether you wish the garment to be light or heavy; use two No. 9 needles. The lace round the jacket is knit first; cast on 113 stitches. First row, purl knitting; second row, purl knitting; third row, knit 2, *slip 1, knit 2 together; draw the slipped stitch over the last knitted one; knit 2, make 1, knit 1, make 1, knit 2, repeat from*; end the row with 1 knit plain. Fourth row, purl knitting; fifth row, like third row; sixth row, purl knitting; seventh row, purl knitting; eighth row, plain knitting; ninth row, same as third row; tenth row, purl knitting; eleventh row, same as third row; twelfth row, purl knitting; thirteenth row, purl knitting; fourteenth row, knit plain; fifteenth row, same as third row; sixteenth row, purl knitting; seventeenth row, same as third row; eighteenth row, purl knitting; nineteenth row, purl knitting; twentieth row, knit plain; twenty-first row, knit plain; twenty-second row, purl knitting (after this row you commence the groundwork and finish the border); twenty-third row, slip 1, knit 1, *make 1, slip 1, knit 1, draw the slipped stitch over the knitted one; (the easiest way of doing this is to draw the second stitch through the first of the two on the left-hand needle and knit it, then take the two off the needle together) knit 1, knit 2 together, make 1, knit 1, repeat from *; repeat this pattern until at the end of the row 3 stitches are left on the needle; then make 1, slip 1, knit 1, draw the slipped stitch over the knitted one, knit 1; twenty-fourth row, purl knitting; twenty-fifth row, slip 1, knit 1, * make 1, slip 1, knit 2 together, draw the slipped stitch over the two knitted together, make 1, knit 3; repeat from *; at the end of the row (last 3 stitches) make 1, slip 1, knit 1, draw the slipped stitch over the knitted one, knit 1; twenty-sixth row, purl knitting; twenty-seventh row, slip 1, knit 1 *, make 1, knit 1, make 1, slip 1, knit 1, draw the slipped stitch over the knitted one, knit 1, knit 2 together; repeat from *; at the end of the row make 1, slip 1, knit 1, draw the slipped stitch over the knitted one, knit 1; twenty-eighth row, purl knitting; twenty-ninth row, slip 1, knit 1, * make 1, knit 3, make 1, slip 1, knit two together, draw the slipped stitch over the two knitted together; repeat from *; at the end of the row make 1, slip 1, knit 1, draw the slipped stitch over the knitted one, knit 1.

Now repeat *twice* the rows from the twenty-second row (which is a purl row) to the twenty-ninth inclusive. Then repeat the third time from the twenty-second row, but this time knit to the end of the twenty-seventh row, instead of to the end of the twenty-ninth, This brings you up to the fifty-second row, a purl row. In knitting this row, knit the first 30 stitches purl, then slip a twine through them drawing out the needle—these stitches are to form one of the fronts; then knit 53 stitches purl in the middle of the row for the back; leave these on the needle, and taking a third needle purl the remaining 30 stitches of the row, which form the other front. Then slip this 30 also on a twine, as you can go on knitting the back more comfortably if you are not bothered by needles holding the stitches of the fronts.

Now for the 53 stitches of the back : Fifty-third row, same as the twenty-ninth. From this row repeat the pattern from the twenty-second row to the twenty-seventh, until you come to the seventieth row; then you work the 8 rows (from twenty-second to twenty-ninth row) again, and decrease 1 stitch at the beginning of each row to form the shoulders. After that row, lift your stitches on to a third needle (or a twine) until you have finished the two fronts. For each front : Work them in the same manner as the back, only decreasing on the inside of each shoulder. Then put all the stitches again on one needle (back and fronts) and knit as before, decreasing once on the shoulders, and taking care to keep the pattern, which by the time you get to this point has become easy to do; work 8 rows. Then knit 2 rows plain for the neck; third row, slip 1, * make 1, knit 2 together, repeat from * ; at the end of the row knit 2; fourth row, plain; fifth row, cast off; now take a crochet-needle and work round the neck and up the two fronts this edge; first row, 1 DC., * 2 chain; 2 treble in the fourth stitch, 3 ch., 2 treble in the same stitch; 2 ch., 1 DC. in the fourth stitch from the last (8th from the beginning), repeat from * and fasten off.

For the sleeve: Begin at the bottom, casting on 25 stitches. First row, purl knitting; second row, purl knitting; third row, * knit 2, slip 1, knit 2 together, draw the slipped stitch over the knitted one, knit 2, make 1, knit 1, make 1, repeat from *, end the row with knit 1; fourth row, purl knitting; fifth row, like third row; sixth row, purl knitting; seventh row, purl knitting; eighth row, plain knitting; ninth row, like third row; tenth row, purl knitting; eleventh row, like third row; twelfth row, purl; thirteenth row, purl; fourteenth row, plain knitting; fifteenth row, plain knitting; sixteenth row, purl knitting; seventeenth row, slip 1, make 1; purl 2 together 12 times. In this row you pass a ribbon for the hand. Eighteenth row, purl knitting; nineteenth row, plain knitting; twentieth row, plain knitting; twenty-first row, purl knitting. Now work five times the jacket pattern from the twenty-second to the twenty-ninth rows, in every fourth row increasing one stitch at each end of the row—before the last stitch and after the first stitch. In the fifty-first row, cast off six stitches, then continue the work; fifty-second row, cast off six, continue the work; in the next row, cast off two stitches at the beginning, and do this every row until you have worked sixty-one rows; cast off the remainder; sew up the sleeve and seam it into the armhole, run a ribbon in round the throat and finish with a bow of ribbon.

BABY'S QUILT IN KNITTING.

Following are directions for a quilt for cradle, knitted in squares of blue and white wool. Use No. 9 needles, and single or double Berlin; pale blue and white are required. Cast on one stitch in blue.—1st row. Wool forward, knit 1; repeat this row five more times, when you would have 7 stitches on the needle.—7th row. Wool forward, knit 2, join the white, knit 3, join on another length of blue, knit 2.—8th row. With blue, wool forward, knit 2, purl 3 in white, knit 3 in blue.—9th and 10th rows. Knit entirely with blue, making a stitch in commencing each row—11th row. Wool forward, knit 2 in blue, 7 white, 2 blue—12th row. Wool forward, knit 2 blue, purl 7 white, knit 3 blue.—13th and 14th rows. Make 1, knit plain, both with blue wool.—15th row. Wool forward, knit 2 blue, knit 11 white, 2 blue.—16th row. Wool forward, knit 2 blue, purl 11 white, knit 3 blue.—17th and 18th rows. Wool forward, knit plain with blue; there should now be 19 stitches on the needle, this completes half the square. You now begin the decreasing.—19th row, with blue. Slip 1, knit 2 together, knit 1, knit 11 with white, knit 4 with blue.—20th row. Slip 1, knit 2 together, knit 1 with blue, purl 11 with white, knit 3 with blue.—21st and 22d rows. Slip 1, knit 2 together, rest plain, all with blue.—23d row. Slip 1, knit 2 together, knit 1 with blue, knit 7 with white, knit 4 with blue.—24th row. Slip 1, knit 2 together, knit 1 with blue, purl 7 with white, knit 3 with blue.—25th and 26 rows. Slip 1, knit 2 together, knit rest with blue.—27th row. Slip 1, knit 2 together, knit 1 with blue, knit 3 with white, knit 4 with blue.—28th row. Slip 1, knit 2 together, knit 1 with blue, purl 3 with white, knit 3 with blue; now finish the square with blue, decreasing each row until you have only 1 stitch on the needle. You join the squares together with blue or white wool, and it has a good effect to arrange the four squares as stars. A knitted border or fringe of blue and white should be added.

BABY'S MITTENS.

Four needles, No. 15, and one skein Andalusian, Shetland, or Split Zephyr wool will be required.

Cast on 40 stitches and knit one row plain.

2d and 3d rounds: Knit 2, purl 2. Repeat.

3d round: Knit 2, wool forward, knit 2 together. Repeat.

4th round: Knit 2, purl 2.

5th round: This and all following rounds are knitted plain.

9th round—the thumb begins now: Knit 2, increase; knit 2, increase. Rest of row plain.

Knit 2 more rows without increasing.

12th round: Knit 2, increase; knit 4, increase. Rest plain.

Knit 2 rows without increasing.

15th round: Knit 2, increase; knit 6, increase. (Remember never to increase anywhere except at this part.)

18th round: Knit 2, increase; knit 8, increase.

21st round: Knit 2, increase; knit 10, increase.

24th round: Knit 2, increase; knit 12, increase.

25th round: Slip the 16 thumb stitches on a piece of wool, leaving them for the present unknitted. Go on with the other part for 24 rounds, then decrease every 5th stitch. Two more rounds, and decrease every 4th stitch. Then two more rounds, and decrease every 3d stitch. Then two plain rounds and cast off, sewing together on the wrong side.

Now go on with the thumb stitches. You must have 18 stitches altogether to make the number right; pick up two at the join. Knit 17 rounds plain.

18th round: Knit 2 together, knit 3. Repeat. Knit 2 more plain rows and cast off.

Crochet a little cuff beginning with 1 chain, 1 double, increasing every round, and scalloping the last.

Increasing is done by knitting two stitches into one, or picking up a loop between two stitches and knitting it. Decreasing is done by knitting 2 together. Rounds not mentioned are of course knitted plain, without increasing or decreasing. In the rounds where the increasings are made, after these have been done, the rest is plain knitting.

WRISTLET PATTERN.

Cast on 6 stitches, 1st row; slip 1, knit 1, make 1, knit 1, make 1, knit 1, make 1, purl 2 together.—2d row: make 3, purl 2 together, knit 1, purl 4, knit 1.—3d row; slip 1, knit 2, make 1, knit 1, make 1, knit 2, make 1, purl 2 together.—4th row; make 3, purl 2 together, knit 1, purl 5, knit 2.—5th row; slip 1, knit 3, make 1, knit 1, make 1, knit 3, make 1, purl 2 together.—6th row; make 3, purl 2 together, knit 1, purl 7, knit 2.—7th row; slip 1, knit 4, make

1, knit 1, make 1, knit 4, make 1, purl 2 together.—8th row ; make 3, purl 2 together, knit 1, purl 2 together, purl 7, knit 2.—9th row ; slip 1, knit 1, slip 1, knit 1, pass the slipped stitch over the knitted one, knit 7, make 1, purl 2 together.—10th row ; make 3, purl 2 together, knit 1, purl 2 together, purl 5, knit 2.—11th row ; slip 1, knit 1, slip 1, knit 1, pass the slipped stitch over the knit one, knit 5, make 1, purl 2 together.—12th row ; make 3, purl 2 together, knit 1, purl 2 together, purl 3, knit 2.—13th row ; slip 1, knit 1, slip 1, knit 1, pass the slipped stitch over the knit one, knit 3, make 1, purl 2 together.—14th row ; make 3, purl 2 together, knit 1, purl 2 together, purl 1, knit 2.—15th row ; slip 1, knit 1, slip 1, knit 1, pass the slipped stitch over the knitted one, knit 1, make 1, purl 2 together.—16th row; make 3, purl 1, knit 1, purl 4. Repeat this pattern until you have a strip long enough to go around the wrist next the hand, 6 leaves will be enough for an ordinary sized hand. Then cast off both ends of the strip together. Take up, on three needles, the stitches of the lower or plain edge and knit 1 plain, 1 purl until the wristlet is of the desired length

RAISED LEAF PATTERN.

The odds and ends of time during the long Summer days can often be used by economic workers, in knitting squares, or shells, or stripes which can afterwards be sewn together into useful and handsome counterpanes, tidies, toilet covers, pin cushions, mats, etc. The coarseness or fineness of the cotton and needles may be left to the taste of the knitter, but as a general rule No. 8 cotton and No. 14 needles may be used for the coarser work, and No. 18 cotton and No. 16 needles for the finer. In every case care should be taken to proportion the cotton to the size of the needles.

A pretty pattern in squares is known as the Raised Leaf pattern, and is worked thus :

Cast on one stitch.
1st row : Over, knit 1.
2d row : Over, knit 2.
3d row : Over, knit 1, over, knit 1, over, knit 1.
4th row : Over, knit 1, purl 3, knit 2.
5th row : Over, knit 3, over, knit 1, over, knit 3.
6th row : Over, knit 2, purl 5, knit 3.

7th row : Over, knit 5, over, knit 1, over, knit 5.
8th row : Over, knit 3, purl 7, knit 4.
9th row : Over, knit 7, over, knit 1, over, knit 7.
10th row : Over, knit 4, purl 9, knit 5.
11th row : Over, knit 9, over, knit 1, over, knit 9.
12th row : Over, knit 5, purl 11, knit 6.
13th row : Over, knit 11, over, knit 1, over, knit 11.
14th row : Over, knit 6, purl 13, knit 7.
15th row : Over, knit 13, over, knit 1, over, knit 13.
16th row : Over, knit 7, purl 15, knit 8.
17th row : Over, knit 15, over, knit 1, over, knit 15.
18th row : Over, knit 8, purl 17, knit 9.
19th row : Over, knit 9, narrow (by knitting 2 together), knit 13, slip 1, knit 1 and throw the slipped stitch over, knit 9.
20th row : Over, knit 9, purl 15, knit 10.
21st row : Over, knit 10, narrow, knit 11, slip 1, knit 1 and throw slipped stitch over, knit 10.
22d row : Over, knit 10, purl 13, knit 11.
23d row : Over, knit 11, narrow, knit 9, slip 1, knit 1 and throw slipped stitch over, knit 11.
24th row : Over, knit 11, purl 11, knit 12.
25th row : Over, knit 12, narrow, knit 7, slip 1, knit 1 and throw slipped stitch over, knit 12.
26th row : Over, knit 12, purl 9, knit 13.
27th row : Over, knit 13, narrow, knit 5, slip 1, knit 1 and throw slipped stitch over, knit 13.
28th row : Over, knit 13, purl 7, knit 14.
29th row : Over, knit 14, narrow, knit 3, slip 1, knit 1 and throw slipped stitch over, knit 14.
30th row : Over, knit 14, purl 5, knit 15.
31st row : Over, knit 15, narrow, knit 1, slip 1, knit 1 and throw slipped stitch over, knit 15.
32d row : Over, knit 15, purl 3, knit 16.
33d row : Over, knit 17, narrow, knit 16.
34th row : Over, knit 16, purl 2, knit 17.
35th row : Over, knit 17, narrow, knit 17.
36th row : Purl throughout.
37th and 38th rows : Narrow, rest plain.

39th row ; Narrow, rest purl.

Continue as from 37th, two plain rows and one purl—always remembering to narrow at the beginning of each row—till there is only one stitch left. Cast off. This completes one square.

In arranging the pattern four leaves should be brought to one point, and the squares should be sewn together as flatly as possible without dragging. The joining of the larger squares thus formed requires no special direction.

TATTING.

Tatting is a strong and durable trimming for undergarments, and in fact for clothing of any kind which it is desirable to wash frequently. It can be made very rapidly, and is not as trying to the eyes as many other kinds of fancy work.

Only two implements are required, a shuttle for holding the thread and a strong pin. If thread is to be used do not get that which is too closely twisted, as it is liable to become knotted in working. Silk tatting is much used for ornamenting flannel garments. Silk is very easily worked, even more so than cotton; the silk to be used is netting silk.

The mode of holding the shuttle and using the hand is of first importance. The shuttle is held lightly between the thumb and first and second fingers of the right hand, and with only a few inches of the thread left loose. Make a loop around the fingers of the left hand, holding it fast by the thumb and forefinger; you are now ready to begin to form your stitches, which is done by letting the shuttle pass under the loop between the first and second fingers, and draw it out towards the right in a horizontal position, when a loop will be formed with the thread which was passed round the fingers of the left hand.

Hold the shuttle steadily in the hand, stretched towards you, while the second finger of the left hand works the loop up to the first finger and thumb, where the loop has been held. *Remember that the stitches are always formed of the loop which passes round the fingers of the left hand.* When a sufficient number of stitches have been made to form a loop the thread is drawn up, and another stitch is formed in the same way as before described.

The clover-leaf pattern is formed by connecting the second leaf through a loop which has been left loose in the side of the first leaf, and so on until the three leaves are formed.

A very bretty border, suited for curtains, toilet covers, skirts, etc., is made by working six of the little scallops and drawing them up

closely to form a star. When a sufficient number of stars have been formed sew them together lengthwise.

The cuts given will show a few of the patterns most commonly used in making tatting.

We give in Cut No. 6, of Tatting Work, an illustration of a very pretty medallion for the end of a tie. When this is made of fine thread it very closely imitates Honiton lace. By a little ingenuity

Cut No. 6.

on the part of the worker, after the stitches are once mastered, very handsome work of this kind can be accomplished in form of barbs, fichus, borders for handkerchiefs, medallions for toilet articles, infants' dress waists, etc., etc.

CROCHET WORK.

Crochet is a kind of knitting done with a hooked needle, and while it is much less intricate than ordinary knitting with straight needles, it possesses the advantage of being better "catch up" work, as it can be hastily laid aside without fear of dropping stitches which often make such trouble for the knitter. It can be worked with the finest thread for imitation lace, and the coarsest double wool for rugs, while there is a large range between for an unlimited variety of useful and fancy articles, such as shawls, counterpanes, slippers, mittens, purses, socks, etc., etc. The material may be cotton, silk, wool, chenile or twine, the object for which the article is to be used determining the material to be chosen.

The stitches which are used in crochet, are chain stitch, slip stitch, single crochet, double crochet, treble crochet, and long treble.

The CHAIN STITCH is the foundation for all others. A single loop is made around the hook or needle, and the thread drawn through this loop, another loop is drawn, and so on, until the required number is made. Chain stitch should be done loosely, as the work afterward being formed to this chain is apt to contract it. It is sometimes desirable, on this account, to make the first chain with a larger needle, particularly for edgings. The first loop placed upon the needle is not counted in making the chain.

SLIP STITCH.—A chain being made the hook is inserted in the last stitch but one to the needle, and the thread is then drawn

through the two stitches, then the needle is placed in the next stitch the same, and so on.

"SINGLE CROCHET" (s. c.) is to insert the needle in a loop of the preceding row, then draw the the thread through both the loop and the stitch at once.

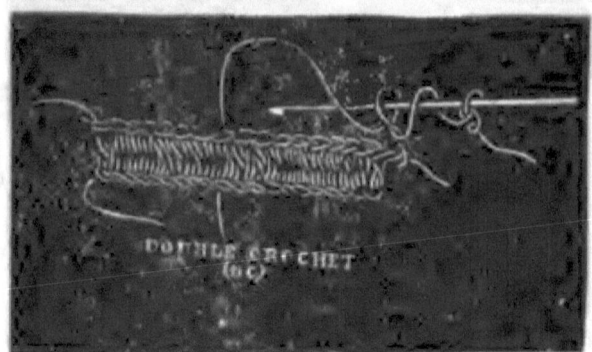

"DOUBLE CROCHET" (d. c.) is to draw the thread through a loop in the lower row, then draw it through the other two stitches.

"TREBLE" (t. c.) is to put the cotton over the needle and insert the latter into a loop; draw the cotton first through the loop, then through two stitches, then again through the last two stitches.

A "LONG TREBLE" (Long t. c.) is the same as the above, except that the cotton is drawn first through only one stitch, then through two, and again through the last two.

In tricoter you make a chain, then pick up each stitch in single crochet; but do not finish working it, only pull it through once, so as to keep every stitch still on the needle. In coming back, pull the wool first through one stitch, then pull it always through two stitches until the row is done. Backwards and forwards count as one row.

To "raise" is merely picking up the stitch from the row beneath, and drawing the wool through in the usual way when doing tricoter.

We give below a few directions for different trimmings and articles which are much used in crochet.

TRIMMING: CROCHET AND MIGNARDISE.

As will be seen from the illustration, this pattern is worked diagonally.

Commence with twenty-one chain, pass over five chain, one treble into the sixteenth, keep the top loop on the hook for the next and following trebles, turn the cotton twice round the hook, work off as for a treble, leaving the top loops of each on the hook; the trebles are worked into every other stitch of the chain; take a length of mignardise,* work a treble as before described into two picots together, repeat from* three times more, work an ordinary treble into the two next picots together, then work off each loop on the hook as one stitch.

2d Row: Four chain (as all the trebles are worked as described in the last row, we shall not repeat the directions), pass over the first treble, one treble into the top of each of the six next successive trebles, one ordinary treble into each of the eight next successive

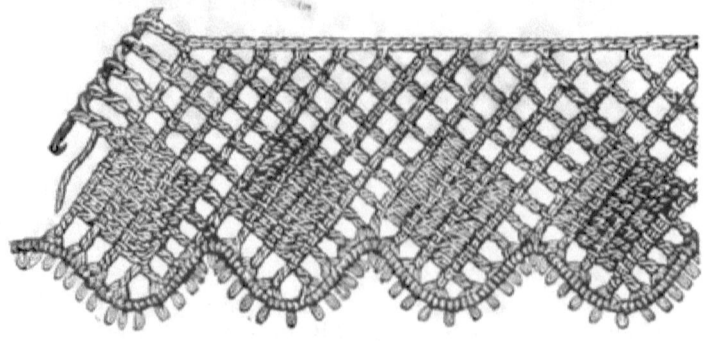

stitches, and one into the two next picots of mignardise together; keep the top loop of each on the hook, and work off as described in the first row.

3d Row: Four chain, pass over the first treble, one treble as described into each of the five next successive stitches, one ordinary treble into each of the eight next successive stitches and into the two next picots of mignardise together; work off as described for previous rows.

4th Row: Four chain, pass over one treble, one treble as described into each of the four next successive trebles, one ordinary treble into each of eight next successive stitches and into the two next picots of mignardise together; work off the same as previous rows. Repeat from the first row, working into the stitches of last row instead of into the chain, as described for first row.

EDGING, CROCHET AND POINT BRAID.

1st Row of Heading: Fold the braid as shown in the design, work six singles into the folded part, six chain, fold the braid again, and repeat.

2d Row: One treble into a stitch of last row, two chain, pass over two stitches, and repeat.

1st Row of Edge: One single into the corner of a fold of braid, six chain, one single into the next corner, ten chain; repeat from the beginning of the row.

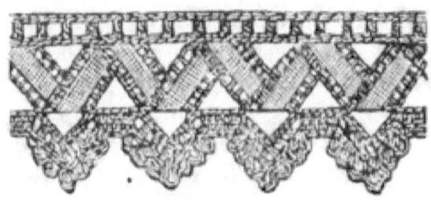

2d Row: One treble into the second of ten chain, one chain, pass over one stitch, one treble into the next, one chain, pass over one stitch, one treble into the next, three chain, one treble into the same stitch, one chain, pass over one stitch, one treble into the next, one chain, pass over one stitch, one treble into the next; one chain, pass over one stitch, one treble into the next, pass over two stitches, one double into each of five next successive stitches; repeat from beginning of the row.

3d Row:* One double into one chain of last row, three chain, pass over one stitch, repeat from * five times more, one double into each of five next successive stitches, three chain; repeat.

TRIMMING: CROCHET AND FANCY MIGNARDISE.

For the center take a length of fancy mignardise, and on the straight side work one double into a picot, four chain, two double trebles into the same picot; keep the top loop of each on the hook and draw through all altogether; pass over two picots, two double trebles into the next picot, keep the top loop of each on the hook and draw through all together, four chain, one double into same picot; repeat from the beginning of the row. Take a length of plain mignardise, work a row like the last; to join the two rows, draw the cotton through the top of double trebles of last row (see design) when working the corresponding trebles on next row.

For the heading on the other side of plain mignardise, work one double, separated by one chain, into each picot of last row.

For the edge of the scalloped side of mignardise work one double into the second picot of a scallop, * two chain, one half treble into the top of last double, one double into next picot. Repeat from * three times more, work into three picots together in the depth of scallop, and repeat.

EDGING: CROCHET AND MIGNARDISE.

For the edge:

1st Row: Two half trebles and two trebles into a picot of mignardise, three chain, two trebles and two half trebles into the same picot, pass over one picot, one single into each of three next picots, pass over one picot, and repeat.

2d Row: One double into center of three singles of last row, four chain, * one double under three chain of last row, three chain, repeat from * four times more, one double under three chain, four chain. Repeat from the beginning of the row.

To join the scallops: Draw through the last loop of three chain when working the first three chain on next scallop.

For the heading : Draw three picots one through the other with a hook (see design), work one double into the last picot, three chain. Repeat.

TRIMMING: CROCHET AND EMBROIDERED BRAID.

White mediæval braid is used for this trimming; it is embroidered with a Greek key design in tent-stitches.

For the crochet edge :—

1st Row: Work one double into two picots together, three chain, one double into the two next picots together, five chain, one double into two next picots together, three chain. Repeat from the beginning of the row.

2d Row: One double into the first double of last row, one chain, seven trebles separated by one chain under the five chain of last row, one chain. Repeat from the beginning of the row.

3d Row: One double into the double of last row, one chain, * one double between the two next trebles, four chain, repeat from * four times more, one double under next chain, one chain. Repeat from the beginning of the row.

For the heading: on the other side of braid work one treble into two picots together, three chain. Repeat from the beginning of the row.

EDGING: CROCHET AND WAVED BRAID.

The loops are made by working with a needle threaded with crochet cotton a single buttonhole-stitch into each point of braid, and passing the cotton on from one point to another.

For the edge: One double into the buttonhole loop, five chain, one double into the same place, five chain. Repeat from the beginning of the row.

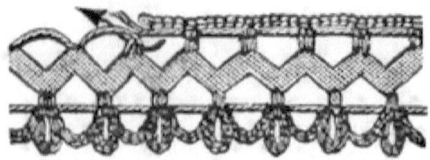

For the heading: One double into the buttonhole loop, four chain. Repeat.

WHITE AND SCARLET SHETLAND SHAWL.

LARGE SIZE.

(9 ozs. white and 2 ozs. scarlet Shetland wool.)

This must be done loosely, with a small ivory or bone crochet-needle.

Make a chain of six stitches for the foundation. Now work three more chain, and do a treble into the fourth from the needle; that is, in the last stitch of the foundation. Do two more treble, one chain, miss one loop, and do three treble; miss one loop and do a treble into the last stitch.

2d row—three chain, two treble, worked into the hole between the first and second stitches; one chain, miss three loops, and work three treble into the next hole; one chain, one treble, into the last loop.

3d row—three chain, two treble, into the first hole, one chain, three treble, into the next hole, one chain, one treble, into the last stitch. You ought now to have formed a small square mat, and henceforth the shawl is very simple. Three treble, one chain, alternately; increase at each corner by working: three treble, one chain, three treble, all into one hole. The first round you will be obliged to work into loops, but after that, into the holes formed by the one chain. As the shawl gets larger, you must do two instead of one chain. For the border, do five rounds in scarlet, then ten in white; then scarlet again for severel inches, and end with a scallop formed thus: one single, one double, one treble, one long treble, two chain, one long treble, one treble, one double. Repeat.

For a smaller shawl you would only require 7 ozs. white wool, but the same amount of scarlet.

LONG PURSE WITH BEADS.

To make this purse it will require four skeins of purse silk and one bunch of beads.

First string on a few beads and commence by making a chain about twelve inches long, then work in long crochet. Place your silk around the needle, put your needle into every other chain stitch, draw the silk through, then through one loop, through two, again through two. Now put forward a bead, then draw the silk through one loop.

Every row after the first, you put your needle through the large hole.

You cut off your silk at the end of each row, and commence at the other end, so as your beads may be all on one side. You crochet up one-third at each end, down in the ends, and add tassels and slide to match the kind of beads used.

LONG PURSE STRIPED.

This purse also requires four skeins, two of each color.

Make a chain ten inches long, work six rows of double crochet, then take the other color, and after it has been joined to the work make a chain of five loops, and join it to the work on every fourth stitch. Next row, you join the chain to the center stitch of the chain in the last row, with a double crochet stitch. When you have worked four open rows, you work one row with only three stitches in the chain, instead of five. Now take the first color and work six rows of double crochet. This forms as you will readily see an open stripe of one color, and a close stripe of the other. You can put beads in on the third stripe, if you desire. String the beads before you commence and put one forward on your thread before you draw it through the work; this purse is made up like the one previously described.

BABY'S SOCK.

Take either Saxony or split zephyr, set up a chain of thirteen stitches, or any uneven number, then crochet around this row, widening at either end and in the middle of one side. Repeat this for about five rows. Then continue crocheting the same only widening in the center alone, until the instep is made. Your own judgment will be the best guide to tell you how deep this should be.

Now you have come to the heel. Divide the piece you have crocheted in half, take up the stitches on the plain half, (not on the piece with the point on it) and crochet in double crochet seven rows or as many as you think will be necessary. Double this heel piece together and join in single crochet. Turn the point over on the front of the sock and take up the stitches in double crochet, and make the stocking in shell stitch, making as many rows as you wish the stocking to be long. You may finish the top with a row of scallops in silk.

Blue and white, or pink, are favorite colors for these socks, or all white, with a ribbon run in around the ankle, which is to be preferred to cord and tassels.

TAM O'SHANTER CAP.

Cast on six stitches, and crochet round these stitches a flat piece, widening at intervals to insure this, and until this head piece is as large as you may desire it, when crochet one round without increasing. Crochet the succeeding rows diminishing in the same proportion as you increased, and work the head band with either increasing or decreasing, taking the stitches through both edges of the loop. Nine or ten rows will be sufficient for this band. It should be crocheted tighter than the other part of the cap.

LADIES' OPERA HOOD.

Take wooden needles about the size of a small pen-holder; get either Pompadour wool or split zephyr, of white or a delicate color. Cast on sixty stitches; knit plain garter stitch, very loose, until you have a piece about fifteen inches long; slip half the stitches (that is thirty), on to a fine hair-pin, and bend it over so they won't slip off; then knit the remaining thirty back and forth until you have made a strip about twenty inches long; bind off. Then go back and take those stitches off the hair-pin on to the needle, and knit back and forth until that strip is as long as the other, then bind off.

Now if you hold the work up it will look very much like a pair of pants, but be not discouraged. Crochet a pretty shell border around the whole thing ; gather and put a tassel on each of the lower ends. Gather the top loosely, and put a large ribbon bow of the same color on top of the gathers and it is done. To wear it, put the part with the bow on just above your front hair, cross the two ends behind and tie them under your chin. It is jaunty and becoming, and will not displace the most carefully arranged hair.

TABLE MATS.

Make a chain of 25 stitches.

DC. all around to the beginning and turn the work. There is one stitch upon the hook ; put the hook back through the last loop through which the cotton was drawn, put the cotton over the hook and draw it through that loop alone ; then put the cotton over the hook and draw through the two loops upon the hook—DC. the row of loops on the back side of the mat to the end.

Crochet twice in each of three adjoining loops at the end, DC. to the other end. Crochet twice in two adjoining loops at that end, bringing the ends of the first row around the mat together. Bring the cotton in front of the hook which has upon it one loop, put the hook through a loop at the end of this row where it commenced, and draw the cotton through the two loops upon the hook joining the row. Turn the work over, put the hook back through the last loop that the cotton was drawn through, put the cotton over the hook, draw through that loop alone, put the cotton over the hook and draw through the two loops.

Crochet twice in the first loop of each of the two loops that had two stitches put in them.

Proceed down the side to the other end—Crochet twice in the first of each of the three loops that had two stitches put in them, then go on to the beginning of the row, join and turn over the mat as before. Continue until the mat is of sufficient size.

For the border pass one loop and make in the second five TC. stitches. Pass one loop and fasten down by DC. in the next, and so on around the mat.

The length of the chain in the middle of course determines the size of the mat. For coffee and tea pots make a chain of six, and fasten together. Crochet twice in every stitch to start the six points for widening.

The cotton suitable is Dexter's No. 6 four threads. A hook small enough to make it very compact should be used. The stitches to be crocheted all the time are upon the back of the mat.

The mat, is worked in ribbed (DC.) crochet, the hook being placed in the outside half of each loop, and the work turned at the end of each round. The increasings are of course, to turn the corners, and the rounds are completed by an SC. before turning back.

A CHILD'S PETTICOAT.

This is worked in ribbed crochet with a bone crochet hook, and the material to be used is pink and white Saxony wool. Begin at the lower edge with a chain a yard and a quarter in length, and divisible by 12, the number for each scallop, which is dented thus:

Work from right to left,* 1 DC. on each of the first 5 ch., 3 DC. into the sixth, for the center and outward peak; 5 DC. on the next 5 ch., miss 2 to shape the hollow or nearer peak; this at the same time makes an open seam, which divides the scallops. Repeat from* and, at the end of the row, to rib the crochet, turn the work, and pierce the needle at the back of the stitch in the preceding line.

At the 20th row decrease by missing 1 stitch on either side of the festoon. Fasten off at the 32d row, and join at the back, leaving a placket hole or not as preferred. Prepare a band of double crochet, on which work any simple crochet edging. A drawing string may be inserted through this.

CROCHETED SLIPPERS.

For a small wool slipper use double Berlin wool, and make a chain of 15 stitches. Work throughout in single crochet, and increase one stitch in the middle of every row for the first twelve rows. This piece forms the front. Now crochet the first 12 stitches backward and forward for thirty rows, and then join to the other side of the front. Pick up the stitches around the top, crochet one row and on the second row work three singles loosely into each stitch. This make a little frill around the slipper. Turn the slipper inside out, line with silk, and sew on a cork sole. Reverse the slipper, pass a ribbon of the same colored silk around underneath the frill, and finish with a bow in front. To make a larger slipper work more rows in front and along the sides. It is a convenience in any case to work to a paper pattern.

BABY'S BIB PATTERN.

Knitting cotton No. 16. Fine bone crochet hook.

Make a chain of thirty-eight stitches, widening in the middle, by making two stitches in the nineteenth loop.

Turn, and double crochet back, always, throughout the work, putting the hook in the outside half of the loop, and widening always in the middle. Continue thus back and forth until you can count fifteen of these ribs, fasten, and break of the cotton.

Then make a new chain of fifty-five stitches, and fasten it with the hook to the upper corner of the piece you have crocheted, opposite the corner where you broke off the thread, to make the rib come right, crochet down the side of the bib, widening at the corner, then across the bottom, widening at the center and at that corner. Then crochet up the other side, and then make a chain of fifty-five stitches without breaking off the thread.

Turn, work back around the bib, and out to the end of the chain on the other side, always widening at the corners and in the middle and always taking the back part of the loop. Continue this until you can count eight ribs on the side, then finish with the shell edge.

The work is done in ribbed crochet.

A SUMMER CLOUD.

A charming Summer cloud may be crocheted of Shetland floss wool worked in shell pattern. A recent specimen intended for seaside wear was of a light blue, nearly three yards long and about two feet wide, and was edged all round with a plain row of scallops, each containing nine trebles. A chain of 361 stitches was first made. This allowed for sixty shells. Each shell was formed of six trebles, the wool being so fine that five trebles failed to make the shell full enough.

The second row was begun by a DC. exactly in the middle of

the first shell of the first row. It was ended by fastening the last shell of the second row in the middle of the last shell of the first row, and finishing with 3 chain.

The third row was begun by making 3 chain precisely in the same hole in which the second row started, and working in this same spot a shell of six trebles, finishing it with a DC. on the middle of the first shell of the second row. At the end of this row, after making a DC. on the top of the last shell of the second row, another shell was worked in the opening at the base of the 3 chain and was finished with a DC. on the top of this 3 chain.

The second and third rows were repeated throughout.

The cloud was worked with a hook about No. 8, and took twelve ounces of the floss.

FEATHER EDGED BRAID TRIMMING.

Fasten the thread to a loop in the braid. Chain seven stitches, put the needle in the second loop from where you commence, draw the thread through the loop and the stitch on the needle, chain four more and fasten in the next second loop, then take up three more loops by putting the needle through each one, and drawing the thread through the loop, and the stitch on the needle, chain four stitches and fasten as before, chain four more and fasten, take up eight loops as the three were taken, chain two and fasten around the last four chain stitches, chain two more and fasten in the second loop from the eight taken up stitches, chain two, and fasten around the next four chain stitches, chain two, and fasten in second loop, then take up three loops, chain two, fasten around the four chain stitches, chain two, fasten in second loop, chain two more, fasten around the seven stitches, chain four, fasten in second loop, double the braid together from this loop, and on the right side of the work, take up a loop of each piece of the braid, draw the thread through these loops, leave the stitch on the needle, and so continue until all have been taken up, as far as the loop above the eight taken up stitches, on the opposite side of the braid, then draw the thread through two stitches at a time until only one stitch remains on the needle, then commence the second scallop same as before. Crochet across the top of the completed edging, to sew on by. And it washes and wears better to crochet a chain of three between each loop on the lower edge, except those close between the scallops, simply drawing the thread through these. The needle must be fine and straight.

ANOTHER PATTERN.

Begin with the third or fourth loop in the braid, bring your thread through and make a stitch, then a chain of three stitches; with the last stitch on your needle bring the thread through the second loop of the braid and the stitches on the needle, counting from the loop you have already taken up, do this three times, then take up every other loop, without making a chain between, five times, then make a chain of three which you join into the center stitch of the last chain you made, make a chain of two and join that to the braid. Repeat this until you have taken up the middle stitch of each of the three chains and joined them to the braid. You find now that you have a scallop filled with crochet, and must join your braid so as to be able to begin another. With one stitch on your needle, double your braid down on the side of your scallop with a loop of the braid in the crease ; now take up two loops (one of each piece) and draw your thread through and keep the stitch thus made on your needle, and continue till you have seven stitches. Now draw the thread through two at a time till you have only one on your needle ; now press open this seam and begin another scallop just as you did the first.

CROCHETED SLEIGH ROBE.

Ten skeins of domestic yarn of four knots each—three-threaded; six skeins bright scarlet, the other four black. Crochet a chain of one of the colors, 51 stitches, or enough to make a strip 12 inches wide, and the length of just two of the skeins. The robe consists of two stripes of black and three of scarlet crocheted together with orange. The Afghan stitch is used. The black strips are to be worked with calla lilies and green leaves, or any other pattern if preferred.

CROCHET ANTIMACASSAR.

This pattern can be adapted for a round couvrette or a square one, and is also pretty done in silk for a sofa cushion. Make a chain of 4 stitches, and unite it. 1st round: Work into 1 loop a long stitch, make 1 chain stitch, work another long stitch into the same place, make 1 chain, repeat. 2d round: 3 long stitches into 1 loop, make 2 chain stitches, miss 1 loop, and repeat. 3d round: 1 double crochet into the 2 chain in last round, make 7 chain, and repeat. 4th round: Into the 7 chain 2 double crochet, 5 long stitches, and 2 more double crochet, and repeat. 5th round: 1 long stitch into the 1st double crochet in last round, make 9 chain, and repeat. 6th round: Into the 9 chain 2 double crochet, * make 4 chain, work 2 double crochet, repeat from * 3 times more, make 5 chain, work a stitch of single crochet into the 2d of the 5, make 1 chain stitch, and repeat from the beginning of the round. 7th round: 1 long stitch into the loop formed with the 5 chain, make 12 chain, and repeat. 8th round: Into the 12 chain 2 double crochet into successive loops, make 4 chain, work 1 double crochet into each of the 2 next loops, make 1 chain, work into the 6th loop 1 double crochet, 5 long stitches, and another double crochet, make 1 chain, miss 1 loop, work 2 double crochet into successive loops, make 4 chain, work 1 double crochet into each of the next 2, make 5 chain, and repeat. This completes the circle. 120 circles sewn together will make a good-sized couvrette, 12 in the length and 10 in the width. If a round couvrette is wished, work one circle for the center larger than the others; this can be done by repeating the 5th and 6th rounds, then sew 8 circles round the center one, and increase the number of circles in each row till you have made it the size you wish. For the square one, tassels are required for the end and sides; these are made by winding the cotton over a cardboard 4 inches deep about 80 times, then twist 8 threads of the cotton into a cord, cut the cotton wound on the cardboard at one end, make 2 inches of the cord into a loop and tie it firmly with the middle of the tassel, then turn it, tie a thread tightly round, about an inch below the cord, and net over the head; 40 of these tassels will be sufficient. Use No. 10 cotton.

RICE-STITCH.

This fancy stitch in crochet is easily learned, and is pretty for shawls, clouds, etc. Make a chain of any length you wish. Wind your thread five times around the needle—put the needle through the 2d loop of the foundation chain—pass the needle under the thread, draw the thread through the loop, and then draw the thread through all the loops upon the needle. This makes a group of threads like grains of rice. Make a chain stitch before proceeding to make the next group. In the next row the groups are to be placed in the chain stitch of the preceding row. This pattern is easily understood.

DEEP CROCHET LACE FOR LAMBREQUIN.

The following pattern is very pretty for a mantel lambrequin, crocheted of seine cord from No. 12 to 20, or of the linen cord which comes for making Macreme lace. The pattern when worked has two rows of open work chain, through which it is very pretty to run bright ribbons corresponding to the room where it is to be used.

The mantel board may be covered with felt, plush, or canton flannel, letting the same come down as a lining underneath the crochet pattern. If the lining and mantel top are of olive, blue, or maroon with ribbons to match run into the open spaces, the effect is very pretty.

To make the fringe for the edge, cut the cord into lengths of say eighteen inches, more or less, according to taste of the worker; make the lengths perfectly even by winding it around a board or book; take two threads at once and fasten by looping into every stitch around the scallops. Nail the work to the mantel board with brass headed tacks, placing them near together and at equal distances apart. Some persons fasten small silk tassels or little balls in occasionally, around the border with the fringe.

Other patterns of crochet edgings given in our book may be found equally pretty to be used in this way.

Foundation chain of 17 stitches.

First row: 1 DC. in 6th stitch from last, 3ch, 3 DC. in 9th stitch; 3ch, 3 DC. in same (9th) stitch fasten down to next stitch of chain, 3 chain, 3 DC. in 15 stitch; 3ch, 3 DC. in same stitch, fasten to the chain; 3ch, 3 DC. in 17th stitch; 3ch, 3 DC. in same stitch; fasten.

Second row: 3ch, 3 DC. in loop made by the 3ch worked between the last 3 DC. in preceding row, 3ch, 3 DC. in same loop,

3ch, 3 DC. in next loop; 3ch, 3DC. in same loop; 3ch, 3 DC. in next or 3rd loop; 3ch, 3 DC. in same loop; fasten, work 6ch, fasten to loop in the last row but one.

Third row: * 3ch 1 DC. repeat from * 5 times, putting all the DC's. in same large loop; then 3ch, 3 DC. in the next loop; 3ch 3 DC. in same loop; 3ch, 3 DC. in second loop; 3ch, 3 DC. in same loop, fasten; 3ch, 3 DC. in 3rd and last loop; 3ch, 3 DC. in same loop.

Fourth row: 3ch, 3 DC. in first loop; 3ch, 3 DC. in same; 3ch, 3 DC. in second loop; 3ch, 3DC. in same; 3ch, 3 DC. in 3rd loop; 3ch, 3 DC. in same; 3ch, fasten over 1st. DC. in large loop: repeat over every DC. in scallop; fasten the last 3ch to little scallop in last large scallop.

Fifth row: Into every loop made on the scallop in last row put 1 SC., 3 DC., 1 SC.; fasten the little scallop down snugly, as much of the beauty of the work depends on their finish; then when you arrive at the body of the work begin again from the first row.

This pattern is quite as effective, and makes a wider border, if the work is done in treble crochet instead of double, one can try a scallop both ways and take their preference.

AFGHAN FOR BABY-CARRIAGE.

It is worked with Saxony wool in alternate squares of white and blue; other colors may, of course, be chosen to suit individual taste. The stitch is crochet tricotee, or what is popularly called "Afghan stitch." Make a chain of 14 stitches with white Saxony wool, making 13 loops of tricotee, work on it 13 rows of white; then take the blue wool, and continue, working 13 rows; then take the white again, working thus in alternate squares until the required length is reached. The next stripe begins with blue wool, and is worked in alternate squares in the same way. The stripes are joined together by a row of chain stitch, in either white or blue; a white square must always be next to the blue ones and *vice versa*. In the center of each square may be embroidered in blue or gold silk, any pretty flower or figure the worker likes. The couvrette is to be finished with a fringe which is crocheted thus—1st row: With white wool, 1 SC. (single crochet) * 7 chain, miss 2 loops, 1 SC. on the next loop, repeat from * all round. 2d row: 1 SC. on the

4th loop of the first 7 ch. (7 chain). 1 SC. on the 4th of the next 7 ch of the preceding row ; continue all round ; this row is worked with blue wool. Next cut the two wools in lengths of 9 inches, and loop 6 strands into the center of each 7 ch. of the 2d row, putting the blue and the white in the alternate chains. Saxony wool is excellent for these Afghans as it washes well, especially if bran is used instead of soap.

AFGHAN STITCH (CROCHET TRICOTEE).

For the benefit of those who may not happen to know the usual Afghan stitch employed in making the above couvrette, a few simple directions may be presented. It is a very easy stitch, and one agreeable to the fingers. The crochet needle must be a rather long one of bone, wood or steel, and the same size from end to end. Holding the wool in the left hand you make with the needle held in the right a running loop or noose ; through this loop draw the wool with the needle making a third loop, and go on thus until your chain has the required number of loops—say seventeen. At the end turn the work back on the chain thus : Put your needle through the 15th loop—the one next but one to the last of the chain—and drawing the wool through leave the stitch on the needle ; with this and the 17th stitch of the chain you will have two stitches on the needle. Put the needle through the next stitch of the chain, and, drawing the wool through, leave the loop also on the needle. Go to the end of the chain thus and you will find 16 stitches on your needle, as in knitting ; in making a chain for crochet tricotee, you must always make one more stitch than the number which the work is to have, as this permits the neat turn at the end. At the end of the first row (all the stitches being on the needle), take up the wool with the hook and draw it through the first stitch only, then catching the wool up again, draw it through the stitch just made and the next stitch on the needle ; then through the stitch just made and the next stitch, and so on to the end of the row, when only one stitch is left on the needle. Then put the hook through the first perpendicular stitch of the preceding row (not the edge stitch), and draw the wool through, leaving the stitch thus made on the needle. Go to the end of the row thus, drawing the wool through each perpendicular stitch of the preceding row, and leaving all the stitches thus made on the needle; then work back as in the second row. This is crochet tricotee, so called because it resembles knitting.

STARS IN CROCHET.

These stars are very useful in many ways. They can be sewed together and made into tidies or doylies, made with fine cotton and sewed together in a long strip, they can be used for the bands of chemises, or for insertion for drawers, underskirts, etc. Made in worsted it makes a very pretty appearance.

Each star is begun in the center by a chain of 8 stitches. In the 1st stitch work 1 treble, * 4 chain, 1 treble in this same 1st stitch, repeat from * 3 times more, 4 chain, 1 slip stitch in the 4th of the 8 chain. You have thus formed 8 rays, joined to the 1st stitch. Now work (without cutting the cotton) the branches, which are begun from the center.

1st branch.—1st round: 18 chain, 1 treble in the 13th, so as to form a purl with the last 5, 2 chain, 3 treble with 2 chain between, missing 2 stitches under the 2 chain, 2 chain, 1 slip stitch in the last of the 18 chain.

2nd round: 2 double over the 1st 2 chain, 2 double with 1 purl between over the next 2 chain, 2 double over the next 2 chain, 1 purl, 7 double over the next 5 chain; then, on the other side of the branch, 1 purl, 2 double, 1 purl, 2 double, 2 double with one purl between, 2 double on the last 2 chain of the branch, 1 slip stitch in the stitch from which the leaf was begun, 5 double over the 4 chain of the circle. Here begins the second branch.

1st round of the 2nd leaf.—22 chain double in the last, so as to form a circle.

2nd round: 1 double in each of the 10 first chain, in the next stitch work 1 double, 1 chain, 1 double to form the point, 1 double in each of the 10 remaining stitches, 1 slip stitch in the 1st stitch of the 1st round.

3rd round: 3 double, 1 purl, repeat from * twice more, then work in double crochet as far as the point, work 2 double with 1 chain between, then work the 2nd half of the branch the same as the 1st. Before beginning the next leaf, work 5 double on the chain stitches of the circle; work 6 branches, repeating alternately the 2 above explained ; cut the cotton and fasten it on again to the point of one of the branches, in order to join them together by the two following rounds :—

1st round : 1 double in the point of one of the leaves, * 4 chain, 1 purl under the chain ; thus make 5 chain, turn the chain with the crochet to the right, insert the needle downwards in the first chain, and make a slip stitch, 4 chain, 1 purl under, 4 chain, 1 purl under, 4 chain, 1 slip stitch in the point of the next leaf, repeat from * five times more.

2nd round : * 4 double over the nearest 4 chain ; 1 purl as usual —that is, above the chain—4 double over the next 4 chain. Now work 1 trefoil (thus : 1 chain, 1 purl, 1 chain, 1 purl, 1 chain, 1 double in the 1 double coming just before the 3 purl), 1 double on each of the next 4 chain of last round, 1 purl, 5 double, 1 trefoil, repeat five times from *.

Join the stars by a few stitches.

For many of the designs in knitting and crocheting, to be found in our manual, we are indebted to the New York *Tribune* extra, and to the *Household*, a paper published in Brattleboro, Vt.

LACE MAKING.

There is perhaps no more beautiful and artistic occupation for women, than that of working lace. It is an industry so fascinating as to engage the lady of wealth, as well as the dweller in the cottage, and a knowledge of this art enables any one of taste to manufacture for themselves many articles of personal adornment, which becomes of double value from being the work of their own hands.

It has been considered that this art is one almost unattainable when in reality it is so simple that any one who can thread a needle, and use it for any kind of fine sewing may as easily make point lace. It is not given to all ladies to possess from their ancestors OLD POINT laces, but by a careful study of this little manual of needlework, they may be able to possess exquisitely worked specimens of MODERN POINT, wrought by their own hands. We shall endeavor to make plain by means of cuts, and diagrams, some of the different stitches, and give such a variety that one can easily take up more intricate work when they desire.

The materials to be used are not expensive or numerous. TRACING CLOTH we mention first, but is only needed by ladies if they desire to copy their own patterns from point lace. A piece of LEATHER or OIL CLOTH, various linen BRAIDS of different widths and kinds, and lace CORDS resembling the satin stitch embroidery. These cords vary in size from a fine crochet cord, to that of a coarse piping cord, and are used in ornamenting the edge of braids and serve as heading to edging; they also are used in light fine work, in place of braids. The thread used in making lace is a fine linen thread and comes in numbers ranging from No. 2, to No. 40, No. 2 being the coarsest, and No. 40 the finest. All these materials and also the patterns traced can be purchased for the different kinds of lace work. Patterns traced on green leather are preferable to those on any other color, as green is better for the eyesight.

We give cuts A, B, C, and 1, 2, 3, 4 as illustrating the braids chiefly used in making lace.

In working begin at the left hand, working from left to right unless in reverse rows. When the braid is cut off, a few stitches should be run through and through the end of the braid to prevent its widening, and when it becomes necessary to join a braid, which

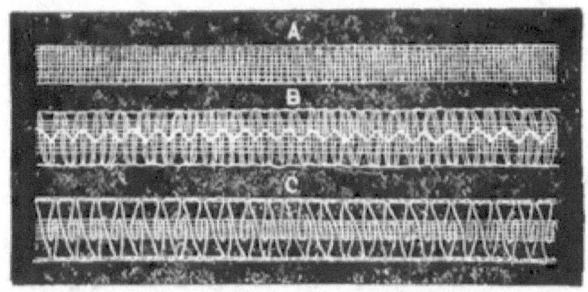

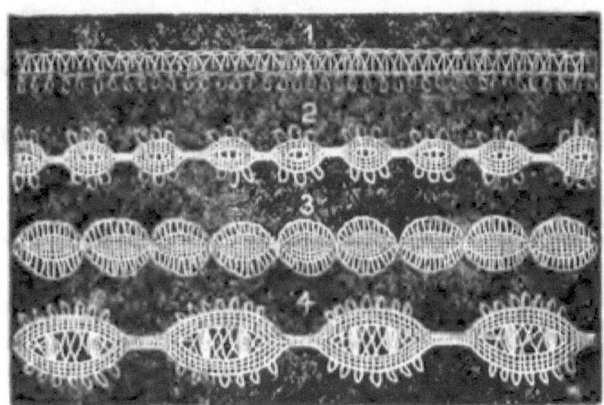

should always be avoided if possible, turn back the ends, sew carefully together over and over, and then stitch down each portion separately. When passing the thread from one portion of the work to another, run the thread through the center of the braid, or where it will show as little as possible, and when commencing the work and in finishing also, it should be neatly and tightly fastened.

The next thing to be considered, and one which is of greatest importance in the work, is PLACING THE BRAID. In cut No. 1 the pattern traced, the mode of tacking on the braid, and the work in process, are all illustrated. The stitches used in "running on" the braid are quite close, as much depends upon keeping the braid smoothly in its place. The braid as will be observed should be

Cut No. 1.

carefully folded over at the points in the pattern, and all the inner parts of the curves should be neatly whipped over and over, as if for fine gathering, and then drawn up to the form of the curve which keeps the braid in place and serves as a part of the work when completed.

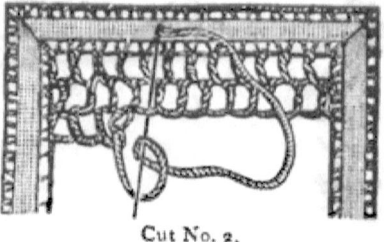

Cut No. 2.

The stitches used are STITCHES PROPER, or points, CONNECTING BARS, FINISHING EDGINGS, WHEELS and ROSETTES. By attention to the following stitches, the rudiments of the art of lace making may be easily acquired, and lovely bits of lace produced, but of course, as will be seen by close scrutiny of specimens of old point lace, there are many more stitches used by the expert lace makers.

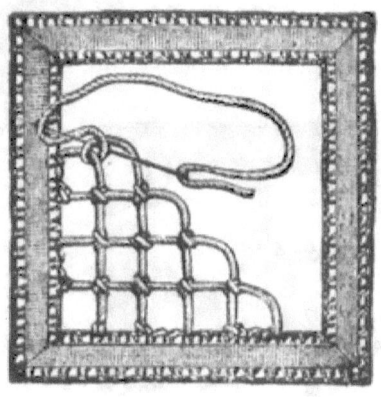

Cut No. 3.

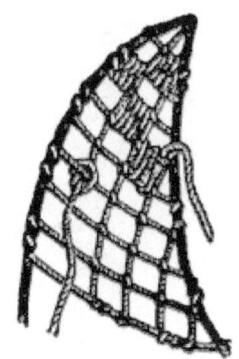

Cut No. 4.

Cut No. 2, POINT D'ESPAGNE (Spanish Point), is worked from left to right. The needle is passed under the stitch, and brought out in front, thus twisting the thread. At the end of each row fasten the thread to the braid, and return by sewing back, putting the needle once in every open stitch.

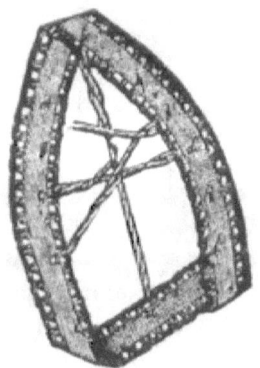

Cut No. 5.

Cut No. 6.

Cut No. 3 is used for groundwork and is very effective, it is called POINT DE FILLET, or net groundwork stitch.

Cut 4 illustrates POINT DE FILLET in conjunction with POINT DE REPRISE, the last named stitch being simply a darning over and under of the bars which had previously been made. This stitch is quickly worked, and an examination of the cuts referred to will give a better idea of the manner of working these stitches than written description could possibly do.

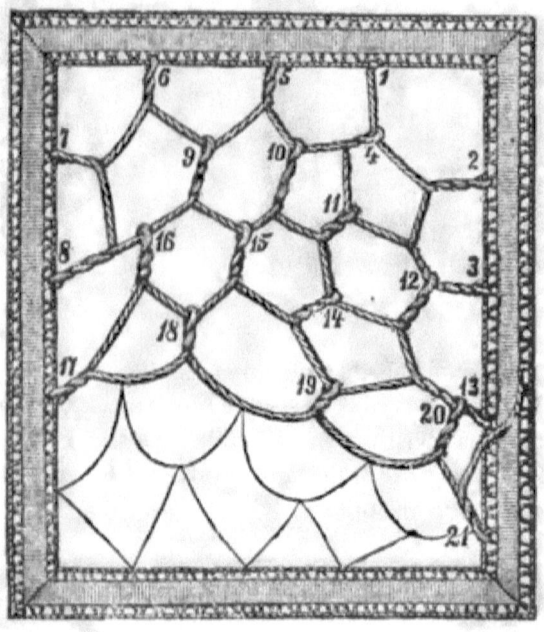

Cut No. 7.

Cuts 5 and 6 represent the SORENTO WHEEL. This is worked by fastening the thread in the pattern to be filled, according to the letters seen in cut 5. Fasten first at the place *a*, then at the place *b*, carrying the thread back to the middle of this bar, by winding it around, then fastening again the thread at *c*, and so on, then the thread is worked over and under the bars as seen in cut 6, which forms the wheel.

RALEIGH BARS are worked over a net work made of thread, (See cut 7) twisted in places so as to make the desired form. After the groundwork is formed these threads are worked over in button hole, or Bruxelle stitch. To form the DOT or PICOT as seen in cut

8, the thread is twisted on the needle the same as in railway stitch (See cut No. 13 in article on fancy needle-work).

The VENETIAN BAR is so simple as hardly to require description. It is worked over two straight threads in button-hole stitch; these bars may be used to fill up spaces in any part of the work where filling is necessary.

Cut No. 8.

MEDALLION IN POINT LACE.

Cut No. 9. This medallion is useful for the ends of neckties, as trimming for jackets, dresses, etc. The mode of working it is quite simple. Place the braid as before directed, work rosette (cut 6) in the center; fill in the open spaces with Point de Fillet (Cut 3) and your medallion is finished.

In Cut 10 is shown a very simple pattern for the end of a necktie. Take braid marked *a*, place upon pattern as before described, and fill in with fine thread, making the center in Sorento wheels, see cuts 5 and 6.

80   MANUAL OF NEEDLEWORK.

Cut No. 10.

HONITON LACE.

Is made of a braid called Honiton braid. The mode of making is much the same as in point lace, the tracing and sewing on the braid being done precisely the same. In cut No. 11 only a few

Cut No. 9.

stitches and twisted bars are introduced, the purl edge must always be used, as the lace braid is of too light a texture to admit of having a heavy edge worked upon it.

Cuts 12 and 13 give two very beautiful designs which can be put to a variety of uses; they give the style of using the braids marked 2, 3 and 4 in combination with the point braids marked A, B and C. The purling on the edge of the work seen in these cuts can be purchased and is run on with a fine thread when the work is finished.

Cut No. 11.

Cut No. 12.

DARNED WORK.

This style of work was done by our grandmothers, and much of the edging for capes, collars and cap borders was worked by their dextrous fingers. Within a few years it has again revived under

Cut No. 13.

the name of Breton lace, which is nothing more or less than a pattern carefully drawn in lace with a fine linen floss.

The same work done on coarse net with coarse cotton is much used for pillow shams, infant's crib and carriage covers, etc., and

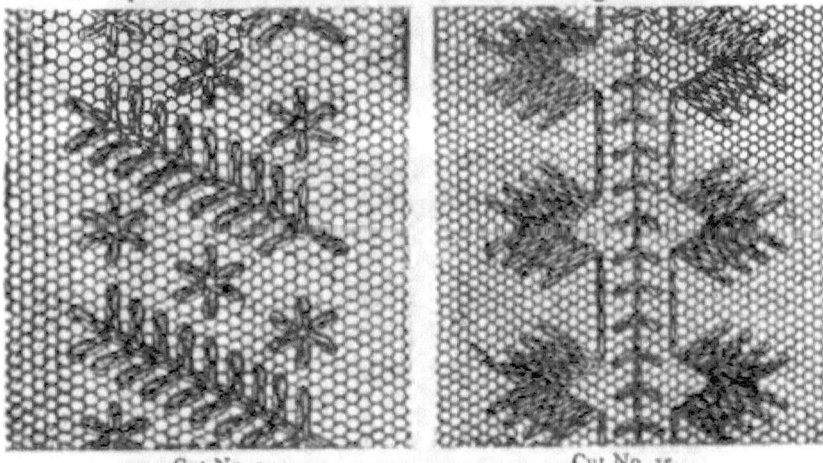

Cut No. 14.   Cut No. 15.

when finished with a bright silk or selicia lining, is very pretty in effect. Cuts No. 14 and 15 will give a better idea of the work than a written description could do.

MACRAMÉ LACE.

The materials for making this lace are, first an oblong cushion, which must be heavy. These look prettiest when made of some bright color, either blue or scarlet, and are best made of silk or Cashmere. The cushion rests on a small table. Two sizes of German pins are also required. The larger size is for pinning on the straight lines at both ends of the cushion, and the small ones are used for putting between the threads on the top line to keep them apart, and fasten the work to the cushion.

The straight lines may be cut the length of the lace required, and should always be double threads; but if cut too short for the purpose, fresh threads may be joined to those, by tying them together with a weaver's knot. The threads for working should be cut to the exact size given with each pattern; but when the required length is not known, cut the threads considerably longer than is necessary, and work out one scallop. Then measure how much the fringe is deeper than required, and cut the next threads shorter by so much. The coarse Italian twine is used in making the lace, when intended for furniture, and the finer twine and linen thread, of various sizes, for dress trimmings or altar linen; the lace is peculiarly adapted to this latter purpose. The lace is also very handsome when made of Maltese silk, either in black or bright colors.

The lace is made by knotting threads together. One thread is held firmly over the other as leader, and each single thread is knotted twice upon it. When a leaf is worked from right to left, the leader is held in the left hand, and when a leaf is worked from left to right, the leader is held in the right hand. Pin on as many straight lines as are required for the pattern.

In commencing a pattern, fasten the threads for working to the top line as follows:—Pass the two ends of each thread under the line, pointing them up, then draw them back through the loop, repeat to the end of the cushion, then put in a pin between every four threads, then loosen the second line, hold it firmly in the right hand, and knot each thread twice upon it with the left hand. The

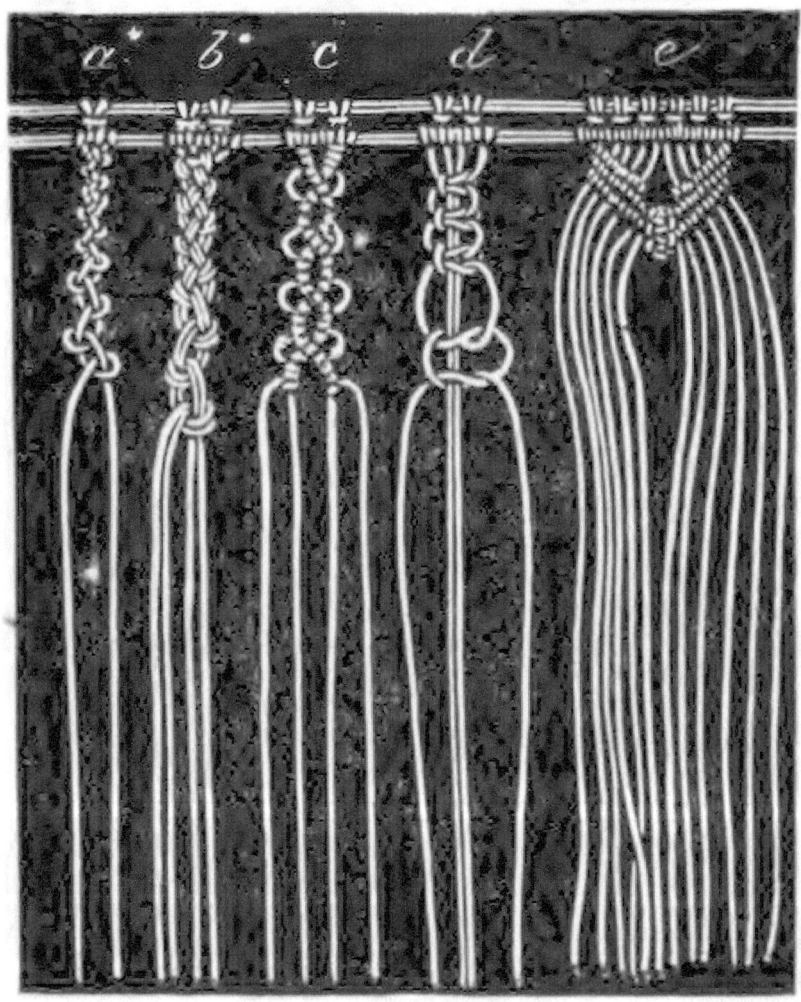

Cut No. 1.

straight lines are always worked in this way. The lace as a rule should be worked tightly, as it adds much to its beauty and durability.

A.—SINGLE CHAIN.

Take two threads, hold one straight in the left hand, knot the other thread to it once with the right hand; hold this thread straight in the right hand and knot the other on to it with the left. Repeat.

B.—DOUBLE CHAIN.

This is made in the same way as the single chain, but with four threads, using two threads each time instead of one.

C.—OPEN CHAIN.

Take four threads, commence with the two at the left side, hold the first of these in the right hand as leader, knot the second twice to it with the left hand, pass the same leader to the left hand, knot the same thread as before twice to it: take the next two threads, hold the first thread in the right hand as leader, knot the second thread twice to it, pass the leader to the left hand, knot the same thread as before twice to it, hold the leader still in the left hand, and knot the first leader twice to it with the right hand; knot the remaining thread at the left side twice to it, leaving a loop before drawing it up tight.* Pass the same leader back to the right hand, and knot the same thread twice to it with the left hand. Then take up the two threads at the right side, hold the under one in the right hand, as leader, knot the other thread twice to it, leaving a loop as before. Pass the same leader to the left hand, and knot the same thread twice to it. Hold the leader still in the left hand, and knot the leader at the left side twice to it; knot the remaining thread at the left side to it, leaving a loop as before. Then pass the leader back to the right hand, and knot same thread twice on to it. Repeat from *.

---

* It would be well to observe that, in making this open chain, after the loops are made, the leader is always passed into the other hand, and the thread knotted twice to it.

D.—SOLOMON'S KNOTS.

Take four threads, hold the two center ones straight; pass the thread at left side loosely over these. Take the thread at right side, pass it over the first thread under the center ones, and up through the loop at the left side; draw it up tight. Then take the right-hand thread, pass it over the two center ones loosely, take the left thread, pass it over this, under the center ones, and up through the loop at the right side; draw it up tight to meet the first part of the knot. This forms one Solomon's Knot.

E.—RAISED PICOT

The raised Picot mostly comes between two leaves. Take the four center threads—two from each leaf—hold the two center ones straight and make six Solomon's knots on to them; pass the two center threads down through the opening between the two leaves; take one of these threads and knot it once to the thread at the left side, take up the other and knot it once to the remaining thread at the *right side*.

NO. 2.

(*Threads for this Pattern one yard and two inches.*)

Pin on the straight lines in the usual way, then fasten on the threads to the top line, after which loosen the second line, and knot each thread twice to it with the left hand. Make a row of Solomon's knots thus:—Take four threads; hold the two center ones straight, pass the thread at the left side over them loosely, then pass the thread at the right side over this, under the two center ones, and up through the loop at the left side; draw it up tight. Then pass the right thread over the two center ones, pass the left thread over this, under the center ones, and up through the loop at the right side; draw it up tight to meet the first part of the knot. Repeat to the end of cushion. Then loosen the third line, hold it in the right hand, and knot each thread twice to it with the left.

FIRST OVAL.—*Take eight threads; divide them into two parts. Begin by holding the fourth thread in the left hand as leader, and

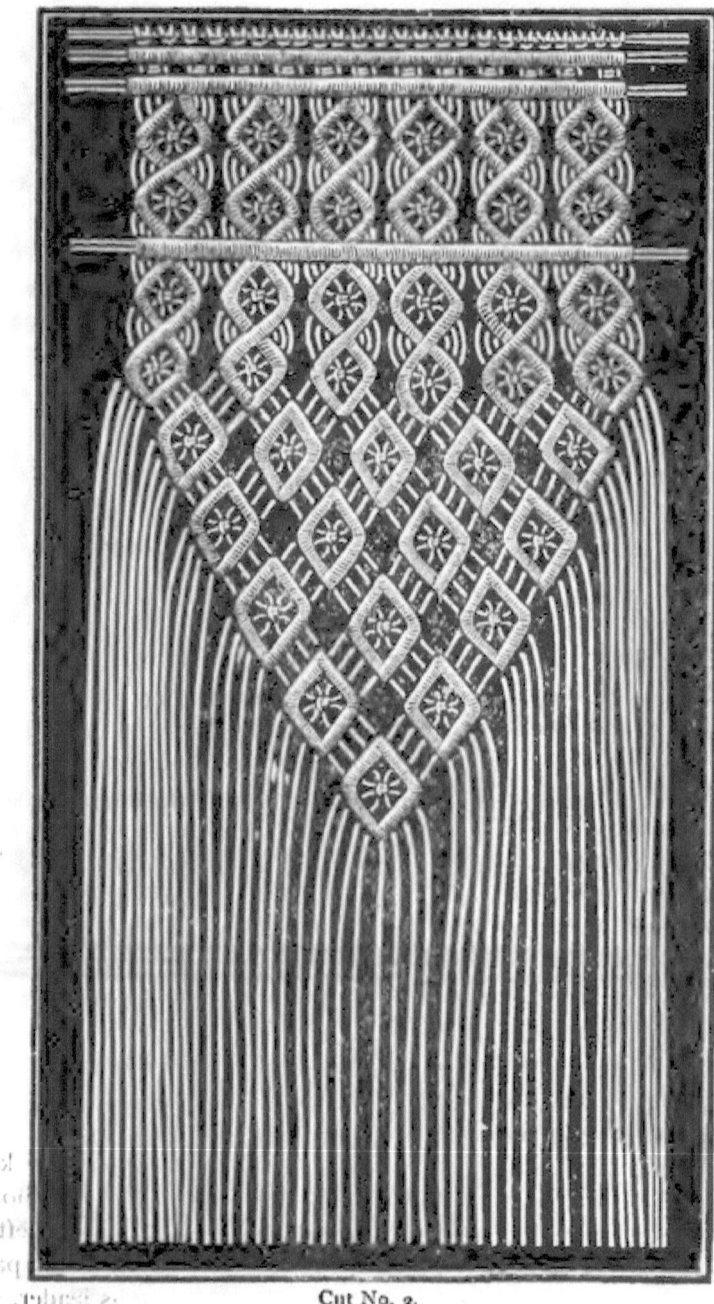

Cut No. 2.

knot each of the three threads twice to it with the right; then take the next four threads, hold the first of these in the right hand as leader and knot the three threads to it with the left hand; then take the two center threads from each side and make a Solomon's knot; then take the first leader, hold it in the right hand, and knot the three threads to it; then take the second thread, hold it in the left hand, and knot the seven threads to it with the right hand. Then divide the eight threads: take the four at the right side, hold the first (at the left side) in the right hand, knot the three threads to it with the left hand; then take the two center threads from each side and make a Solomon's knot; then take the leader at the right side, hold it in the left hand, knot three threads to it; then take the leader at the left side, hold it in the right hand, and knot the remaining three threads to it with the left hand. Repeat from * to the end of the cushion. Then loosen the fourth line, hold it in the right hand, and knot each thread twice to it with the left hand. Repeat this to the end of the cushion; and for the scallop, take eight threads and repeat from * six times. Then take the top leader from the second oval, hold it in the left hand, and knot the four threads of the first oval to it with the right hand; then take the top thread at the left side, hold it in the right hand, and knot the three threads of the second oval to it. Then make a Solomon's knot in the middle with the four center threads; then take the leader at the left side, hold it in the right hand, and knot three threads to it with the left; then take the leader at the right side, hold it in the left hand, and knot the four threads to it with the right. Repeat until there are five small ovals; then make four under these in the same way, and three under the four—and so on—to form the scallop, until it comes to one. If preferred, the fringe may then be knotted, which gives it a rich effect.—See No. 4 Pattern.

NO. 3.

(Threads for this Pattern one yard three inches long.)

Pin on the straight lines in the usual way, after which fasten on the threads thus:—Pass the two ends of each thread under the top line, pointing them up, then bring them through the loop, then loosen the second line, hold it in the right hand, and knot each

thread twice to it with the left hand. Then take two threads:
hold the first in the left hand, knot the other three times to it
with the right hand; repeat this to the end of the cushion. Then
take one thread from each: hold one in the right hand, and knot the
other to it with the left hand; repeat to end of cushion. Then
loosen the third line at the right side, hold it in the right hand, and
knot each thread twice to it with the left hand. *Take the first

Cut No. 3.

six threads, hold the first thread in the right hand as leáder, knot
the five threads to it with the left hand, each thread twice; then
make the second row of the leaf thus:—Hold the first thread at the
left side again in the right hand, knot each of the five threads twice
to it with the left hand; then take the next six threads, hold the
sixth thread in the left hand as leader, and knot each of the five

threads to it with the right hand: then make the second row of the leaf by holding the sixth thread again in the left hand and knotting each of the five threads to it with the right; then hold the same thread as leader in the left hand, and knot the leader of the first leaf twice to it; then make the third leaf, hold the same leader still in the left hand, and knot the threads to it with the right hand; then take the six threads and repeat for a second line; then take the six threads at the right side, hold the first of these (that is the left side one) in the right hand and make the fourth leaf, knotting the threads on with the left hand; repeat for the second line; repeat from * to the end of the cushion; then loosen the fourth line, and knot each thread twice to it in the usual way.

*FOR THE SCALLOP.—Take eight threads, divide them into two parts; take the first four threads, hold the first thread in the right hand, and knot the three threads to it with the left hand. *Second Row of Leaf.*—Take the first thread again, hold it in the right hand and knot the three threads on with the left hand; then take the next four threads, hold the fourth thread as leader in the left hand, and knot each of the three threads to it with the right. Make the second row of the leaf in the same way; hold the leader still in the left hand, and join the two leaves by knotting the leader of the first leaf twice to it. Repeat from * six times, then reduce it one in each row until the point is formed according to the engraving; then join the two leaders of the leaves at the point; then take the first thread at the left side, hold it in the right hand as leader, and knot each thread three times to it down the side of the scallop to form a continuous line; then take the thread at right side of the scallop, hold it in the left hand, and knot each thread three times to it with the right hand; then join the two leaders by holding one tight and knotting the other twice to it; then take the first thread again at the left side and make a second line, after which take the first thread at the right side, hold it in the left hand and make a second line; repeat at each side to form a third line. The leader is always held at the top, and the threads underneath, after which the threads are all held back, fastened down with a needle and thread on the wrong side, and then cut close.

NO. 4.

(Threads for this Pattern to be one yard long.)

Commence by pinning on the straight lines in the usual way, after which fasten on the threads for working, to the top or first line. Pass the two ends of each thread under the line, pointing them up, then draw them through the loop; then loosen the second line at the right side, and knot each thread twice to it with the left hand. Then make a row of Solomon's knots with every four

Cut No. 4.

threads to the end, after which loosen the third line, and knot the threads to it as before. Then take four threads and make three Solomon's knots with them. Repeat to the end of the cushion. Then loosen the fourth line, and knot each thread twice to it with the left hand, as before; then take the first four threads, hold the first of these in the right hand as leader, at the top, and knot the three threads to it with the left (each thread twice); then pass the same leader to the left hand, and knot each of the three threads to it with the right. Repeat this five times. Then make two more chains, exactly the same as last. Then take six threads: hold the first in the right hand as leader (the leader should always be at top, and the threads underneath), and make a leaf of two rows; then take the next six threads: hold the one at the right side in the left hand as leader, and make a leaf of two rows; then take the two center threads of each leaf, and with them make a row of six Solomon's knots; then pass the two center threads of these four between the two leaves, pointing them down, and knot these threads to the other two, to form the raised Picot. Then take the center thread at the left side, hold it in the left hand as leader, and knot the threads on with the right hand, to make the lower leaf at the left side (two rows); then take the center thread at the right side, hold it in the right hand as leader, and make the lower leaf at the right side; then make three more chains, and then another star of four leaves, with raised Picot in the center. Repeat to the end of cushion. Loosen the fifth line, and knot each thread twice to it, as before. Take four threads, make three Solomon's knots with these. Repeat to the end of cushion. Loosen the sixth line, and knot each thread twice to it, as before; then make a row of Solomon's knots with every four threads; then loosen the seventh line, and knot each thread twice to it, as before.

TO FINISH OFF THE INSERTION.—Keep the last line pinned on at both ends; take two threads, draw the second one up under the line in a loop, pass the ends of both threads through this loop, draw them up tight, to form a knot, same as the one at the top line. The two threads will now be in front, between the two last lines. Pass these threads to the back, one at each side of the knot, tie them firmly together at the back; sew these threads neatly to the work, on the wrong side, with a needle and thread. Repeat to the end of cushion, and then cut the threads close.

RUG-MAKING.

TURKISH OR PERSIAN RUGS,

or at least as *handsome*, and in designs *like* the real imported rugs, can now be made in your own home. They are quickly made, and the designs can be bought all ready for working, or if one does not

care to go to the expense of buying them already marked, and has taste and skill in designing, they can draw their own patterns.

The designs as purchased consist of animals, flowers, Persian and Turkish figures. They are on burlap or jute cloth, and so plainly marked in all the colors required that the most inexperienced can readily make good work. They can be filled in with various kinds of wool rags, or wool yarn. A hook is used in drawing in, which is made expressly for the purpose, and when the work has been neatly clipped or sheared off they imitate very closely the best Turkish rugs.

The material used as a foundation for these rugs, as before mentioned, is burlap or jute cloth. The frame for holding the rug while being worked is composed of four strips of board about two inches wide, and about one inch in thickness. This frame can be nailed together at the ends the size needed for the work, and then placed upon the backs of four chairs; it can be easily obtained however remote the person may be from city or town. A regular frame supported by legs can be made by any carpenter, but the one mentioned above is just as well for ordinary use.

The burlap or foundation should be strongly hemmed before sewing it to the frame, which is done with a strong twine; the stitches in sewing in, should not be over one inch apart, as the pattern requires to be held firm and even, as all irregularities will show when the work is finished. The threads in the burlap are not always regular, but this will make no difference if the pattern is held firm and fastened securely and squarely to the frame. If the material used to work with is thick cloth or flannel, it should be cut about one quarter of an inch in width, but thin cloth may be used double that width, and folded together so as to make it about the same width as the other. Cotton rags, of course, can be used, but are not desirable as they so readily change color. There is no directions to be given in regard to the length of pieces required in drawing in, as any length can be used, even that which will hook through twice. The cloth should be held underneath the pattern, and the hook should pass through the burlap from above, drawing the material up through with the hook, leaving a loop about one quarter of an inch above the pattern, then, after leaving about two threads of the burlap between, the hook is again passed through and drawn up as before. Continue this until the piece is all used, always drawing the end of the piece through on the top, and the material close to the burlap underneath. It is well to draw in the outline of the figures first, then fill them in, before doing the groundwork, and it is also much better to clip or shear the work as it progresses, as you are more likely thus to keep it even.

If yarn is to be used instead of cloth or flannel, place several threads together, but do not twist them, and work the same as with rags, it will require from three to six threads according to the size of the yarn used.

Taste and judgment in the use of colors must be used, if the designs are drawn at home, but if the patterns are purchased, the colors to be used are all imprinted upon them. The taste of the worker may even then dictate other colors than those which are stamped, so as to utilize material which they may have on hand; in *this* work as in *all* work much depends upon individual taste, and very handsome rugs may be thus executed with comparatively little expense.

While writing of rugs, a very pretty rug may be made by raveling out pieces of old tapestry carpets. The carpet is first cut into strips of equal widths (say a finger in width), and raveled, taking care that in raveling the threads are kept evenly together. Then take a piece of burlap the size you wish your rug, lay a double row of the threads raveled on one end, and with your sewing machine and a coarse cotton, stitch through, and back again. Then lay back the inner part of the row stitched on, and place another row of stitching as before, the stitching should be about one inch apart. This makes a pretty soft looking rug. The same may be done by hand, but these rugs of course are not as durable as the Turkish rugs before described.

KNITTED RUGS.

Another very pretty style of making rugs and one in which many elderly ladies delight, because of their love for knitting work, is to take the threads of remnants of tapestry Brussels carpets (these remnants can be purchased at the carpet stores), raveling, as before described, and then knitting them into a rug as follows :

Take No. 8 crochet cotton, and No. 12 knitting needles, cast on 30 stitches more or less, and knit three times across. *Then slip 1 stitch, knit 1, put 1 of the worsted threads over the right hand needle, carefully doubling the thread so it shall come precisely in the middle, that the ends may be of equal length, knit the 3d stitch, put on another thread of worsted, repeat until the last two, which are knit plain. Next row slip 1, knit 1, take up the worsted and 3d stitch together and knit as 1 stitch, continue to knit thus, taking the worsted and cotton together in every stitch across. Repeat from * alternating in this way until your strip is the length required. Three of these strips with a border added of about one-half the width of one strip, makes a large-sized rug. Sew the strips together over and over, or crochet them together on the back. It is much easier to knit in strips, as the work becomes heavy. It produces a good effect to knit the center strips in variegated or mixed colors, and the border plain black, or some dark color.

Many persons cut cloth or flannel into narrow strips, say one-fourth of an inch wide and 4 or 5 inches long, (or goods of any kind can be utilized in this way that does not fray too much, cut the thinner material a little wider), and knit the same as with the worsted ravelings.

Turkish Rug Patterns.

Turkish Pattern No. 131.

OUR PATTERNS ARE TURKISH.

Animal, Flower, Scroll, and other designs, printed by hand on suitable jute cloth, (burlaps) and are shaded in the various colors required to make them perfect. The designs are not on paper, but cloth which forms the body of the rug, and are so plain that a person with very little practice can fill them readily and make good work. They are filled with various kinds of rags or wool yarn, with a hook we make expressly for the purpose, and the surface is clipped or sheared off, leaving about a quarter of an inch rising above the pattern, like the best Turkish Rugs, and when well made they are equally handsome, and will outwear four ordinary carpet rugs. They are splendid for needle-work—cross stitch—for the close attention required for transferring designs from paper patterns is all saved, but the hook work is more rapid and much more durable.

Pattern No. 19.

DESCRIPTION OF DESIGNS AND RETAIL PRICES.

No. 7. ⅞ yards wide by 1¼ yards long. A large lion lying down and a small lion in the back-ground, with a fine scenery of flowers and palm trees. Is very easy to work, and makes a nice hearth rug. Price, 95 cents.

No. 61. ⅞ by 1½ yards. A very pretty center, consisting of *full blown* roses, buds, leaves, lilies and various other flowers, surrounded by an oval wreath of flowers extending the whole length of the rug, with the Odd-Fellows' emblem of three links entwined with leaves in the corners, making one of the finest patterns. Price, 95 cents.

No. 22. ¾ by 1½ yards. A very pretty scroll border, with a stag standing near a lake of water, very pretty landscape, scenery, etc., in the center. A very nice sofa rug. Price, 85 cents.

No. 39. ¾ by 1½ yards. A cat and three kittens playing on the carpet in the center, enclosed in a plain scroll. Plain border with nice scroll in corners. A very interesting design for those who are fond of *our pets*. All new. Price, 85 cents.

No. 51. Size and border same as No. 39, with a choice cluster of roses, leaves, buds, etc., in center   Price, 85 cents.

No. 90. ¾ by 1½ yards. Plain border with Grecian corners, choice cluster of flowers in center, surrounded by a nice scroll. Plain, but extra new design Price, 85 cents.

No. 91. ¾ by 1½ yards. Same border and scroll as No. 90, with a large dog and landscape scenery in the center. Price, 80 cents.

No. 76. ¾ by 1¼ yards. A Grecian border in red and black, with solid clusters of flowers of all kinds in center. This makes a handsome mat, and is so simple the most inexperienced worker can make it easily. Price, 75 cents.

No. 36 ¾ by 1¼ yards. A wreath of leaves with scrolls in corners of border, and a Spaniel dog (life size) lying on a carpet of diamonds in center. Very easy to work. Price, 70 cents.

No. 96. ¾ by 1¼ yards   A pretty scroll in red, brown and black, with a cluster of roses, leaves, buds, etc., in center. Makes a very handsome rug. Price, 70 cents

No. 95. Size and border same as No. 96, with a large cat on ottoman in center. Price, 60 cents.

No. 52. ⅔ by 1⅛ yards. Scroll border, a horseshoe in each corner and a horse's head in center. All new. Price, 55 cents.

No. 24. ⅔ by 1⅛ yards. A rustic border in three colors, with pretty openings, forming a frame for a picture of a life-size cat lying on a green carpet. The border is entirely new, and the whole pattern is easy to fill. Price, 55 cents.

No. 45. ⅔ by 1⅛ yards. A border of autumn leaves with a wreath of flowers in center. Easy to fill and very desirable. Price, 55 cents.

No. 44. Size and border same as No. 45, with dog of No. 19 in center. New arrangement. Price, 55 cents.

No. 80. ⅔ by 1⅛ yards. A plain border with Grecian corners, and a stag head in center. A splendid design for a door mat. Price, 55 cents.

No. 93. ⅔ by 1⅛ yards. A nice floral center, consisting of red and moss roses, leaves, buds, lilies, etc., beautifully arranged, with a plain scroll surrounding the center, and three autumn leaves in each corner, and a plain border. Price, 55 cents.

No. 43. ⅔ by 1¼ yards. Same border and center scroll as No. 40, only the scroll is enlarged and the half wreath is left out. A new floral center, composed of roses, pansies, bell flowers, buds, lilies and leaves. All new. Price, 55 cents.

No. 40. ½ by 1 yard. A rose and leaves in each corner; a border in shades of red, brown and orange; a neat flower center surrounded by a handsome scroll ; a rose and leaves forming a half wreath at each end between the scroll and border. All new. Price, 45 cents.

No. 19. ½ by 1 yard. A Spaniel dog lying on a box, very clearly printed in moss and brown colors in center. A branch with roses, leaves and buds at each end, and a plain border. Price 45 cents.

No. 49. ½ by 1 yard. A very neat scroll border with a cat lying on ottoman in center. Very plain and easy to work. Price, 45 cents.

No. 63. Same size and design as No. 40, except the Odd-Fellow's emblem of three links, with letters F.L.T. enclosed, is in each end in place of the half wreath. Price, 45 cents.

No. 97. ½ by 1 yard. A plain border in two colors, with small cluster of flowers in corners with a center piece of flowers and scroll work. This pattern once seen speaks for itself. Price, 45 cents.

No. 98. ½ by 1 yard. Same border as No. 97, with a very pretty wreath of morning glories, roses, bell flowers, etc., for a center. Price, 45 cents.

No 75. Size, border and center scroll same as No. 97, with Free Mason's emblem in center. Price, 45 cents.

No. 66. 4-9 by ⅝ yards. Plain border with a small scroll in corner, a center of flowers, etc. This was designed for a carriage or sleigh mat, but looks well wherever you put it. Price, 35 cents.

No. 79. 4-9 by ⅞ yards. A plain border, with a small cluster of flowers surrounded by plain scroll work in center. A nice carriage or door mat. Price, 35 cents.

The following patterns are *very choice* new Turkish designs, with groundwork and all colored:

LATEST STYLES.

No. 130. ½ by 1 yard. Turkish design. Price, 50 cents.
No. 131. ½ by 1 yard. Turkish design. Price, 50 cents.
No. 136. 4-9 by 1 yard. Turkish design. Price, 45 cents.
No. 140. ⅔ by 1¼ yards. Turkish design. Price, 60 cents.
No. 150. ¾ by 1¼ yards. Turkish design. Price, 70 cents.
No. 160. 1 by 2 yards. Turkish design. Price, $1.40.
No. 170. ⅞ by 1¾ yards. Turkish design. $1.20.

OTTOMAN AND FOOT-REST PATTERNS.

No. 2. 14 by 20 inches. Plain oval border in red and black, a branch of full and half-blown roses, leaves and buds, in center. Price, 20 cents.

No. 3. 20 by 20 inches. Octagon border, and a floral center of pansies, rose, bell flowers, leaves and buds. All new. Price, 25 cents.

No. 5. 20 by 20 inches. Plain black and red border, formed of eight quarter circles; a rose with green and autumn leaves around it for a center. Price, 25 cents.

No. 6. A cat's head for a center. Price, 25 cents.
No. 7. A dog's head for a center. Price, 25 cents.
No. 9. A new and very pretty floral center. Price, 25 cents.

Nos. 6, 7 and 9 are the same size and border as No. 5, and can be filled out either square, round or octagon, and are also nice for chair cushion covers.

Retail price of rug-hooks, 25 cents. Clamps, 50 cents per set of four. Perfect skein, all wool carpet filling yarn, $1.00 per lb. We do not keep waste carpet yarn now, for it is in too short pieces to be worth using.

NEW PATTERNS.

No. 160. ¾ by 1½ yards. Turkish design. Price, $1.40.
No. 41. ½ by 1 yard. A floral center of red roses, buds, pansies, lilly, bell flowers and leaves, surrounded by a scroll in brown and orange, and a plain border. Price, 50 cents.

GOODS BY MAIL.

To favor those not able to get our patterns and hooks otherwise, we send them by mail, postage paid, on receipt of price named. Yarns by mail must have 17 cents per lb. extra, and clamps 25 cents per set, extra, to pay postage. Send money in a registered letter or post-office order, and it will reach us safely. Money in common letters is at sender's risk.

TERMS—C. O. D. (cash on delivery.)

☞ CANVASSERS WANTED. ☜

Address, **PATTEN PUBLISHING COMPANY,**
47 BARCLAY STREET, NEW YORK.

WAX FLOWERS WITHOUT A TEACHER.

The growing taste for making WAX FLOWERS, and the difficulty which we know people in country towns experience, and the expense they often incur in learning the beautiful art, and in obtaining the material and tools to work with, has given us the idea of putting up the materials and tools in boxes, with complete instructions for making WAX FLOWERS and LEAVES to accompany each box. These instructions will be so plain, concise and practical, that persons of ordinary ingenuity and good taste will have no trouble in constructing by them all kinds of leaves and flowers, and even forming elegant bouquets, wreaths, crosses, etc., etc. In order to introduce the knowledge of constructing Wax Leaves of all description, and to initiate the beginner in the art of molding the wax, we have put up and have now ready

Box No. 1.—IVY LEAVES.

Containing different shades of green wax, brass mold, together with wire, instructions, etc. A complete outfit for constructing several fine vines of Ivy Leaves.

PRICE BY MAIL, POST-PAID, FIFTY CENTS.

Box No. 2.—AUTUMN LEAVES.

Now ready, contains a variety of different colored wax, brass molds, molding tools, color in bottles, wire, brushes, etc., with instructions for making a variety of AUTUMN LEAVES, and all in sufficient quantity to make several groups of each kind.

PRICE BY MAIL, POST-PAID, $2.50.

Box No. 3.—VARIETY OF FLOWERS.

Contains wax of different colors, brass leaf molds, molding tools, colors in bottles, wire, brushes, etc., in sufficient quantity to make several Fuchsias, Lilies of the Valley, Pansies and Blush Roses, etc.

PRICE BY MAIL, POST-PAID, $2.50. [See next page.]

Box No. 7.—POND LILY.

This box contains material for making a number of pond lilies and leaves. It consists of white and two shades of green wax—thick and made for this particular use—papers of coloring matters, bloom, brush, wire, molding pin and pond lily brass leaf mold.

PRICE, $1.25.

WAX FLOWERS
—AND—
FRUIT MODELING
WITHOUT A TEACHER.
With Illustrations and Diagrams.

A PRACTICAL TREATISE ON THE ART OF MODELING AND COLORING WAX SO AS TO IMITATE ALMOST ANY KIND OF FLOWER OR FRUIT.

ALSO

Teaches How to Make Wax Leaves, Crosses, etc.

PRICE 25 CENTS.

The above is the title-page to our book on Wax Flower Modeling, etc., and indicates the scope and design of the work. It is written by a practical worker in wax, and is so plain that, by its use, almost anyone can, without other teaching, learn to make Wax Flowers and Fruit. In fact, several persons, to our knowledge, have become successful teachers of the art without any other instruction than what they obtained from the pages of this book.

It will be sent FREE with every order for Wax Material amounting to $1.50, and will also be sent free with each of the **above boxes**, except the Box No. I.

Address **PATTEN PUBLISHING CO.,**
47 Barclay Street, New York.

BEAUTIFUL BOOKS FOR LADIES.

LADIES' FANCY WORK.—A charming book, devoted to Feather Work, Paper Flowers, Fire Screens, Shrines, Rustic Pictures, a charming series of Designs for Easter Crosses, Straw Ornaments, Shell Flowers and Shell Work, Bead, Mosaic, and Fish Scale Embroidery, Hair Work and Cardboard Ornaments, Cottage Foot Rests, Window Garden Decorations, Crochet Work, Designs in Embroidery, and an immense variety of other Fancy Work to delight all lovers of Household Art and Recreation. Price, $1.50; gilt, $2.00.

HOUSEHOLD HINTS AND RECIPES.—This is not a Cook Book but a valuable little book devoted to house-keeping topics, and full of useful items, hints and directions about the house in all its departments, from the kitchen to the parlor, bed-room and attic. It contains a wonderful amount of real good practical information about housework, and there are recipes by the hundred so valuable that no prudent housekeeper can afford to be without them. A single hint may save her many dollars in money, or much wasted time and trouble. Price 50 cents, paper covers.

FRET SAWING FOR PLEASURE AND PROFIT.—WILLIAMS' HAND-BOOK OF INSTRUCTIONS IN FRET SAWING.—This new book is full of valuable information to all who are interested in Fret Saw Work, and contains a multitude of complete and practical directions how to become successful in the use of the Scroll Saw, large or small, and all the other accompanying tools. The following list of contents will give a fair idea of its character: Hints on Materials, Saws (hand and foot-power), Saw Frames, Treadle Machinery, Tools and Implements, Glue Polish, Sand Paper, Paste, Using Fret Saw Designs, Marquetry, Wood Carving, Overlaying, Cutting-Out Work, Beveling Edges, Putting Work Together, Warping of Wood, Inlaid Work, the Pleasure and Profit of Fret Sawing, etc. In addition there are given numerous illustrations and designs of fancy articles, and of all materials explained in the directions. In appearance the book is exceedingly handsome, of unusually handsome decorations, and in price it is the cheapest of all publications relating to the subject. Price by mail, post-paid, 50 cents, paper covers; $1 cloth.

HOUSEHOLD ELEGANCIES.—A splendid book on Household Art, devoted to a multitude of topics interesting to ladies everywhere. Among the most popular topics are: Transparencies on Glass, Leaf Work, Autumn Leaves, Wax Work, Painting, Leather Work, Fret Work, Picture Frames, Brackets, Wall Pockets, Work Boxes and Baskets, Straw Work, Skeleton Leaves, Hair Work, Shell Work, Mosaic, Crosses, Cardboard Work, Worsted Work, Spatter Work, Mosses, Cone Work, etc. Hundreds of exquisite illustrations decorate the pages, which are full to overflowing with hints and devices to every one, how to ornament their home cheaply, tastefully, and delightfully with fancy articles of their own construction. By far the most popular and elegant gift book of the year. 300 pages, 265 illustrations. Price, $1.50; gilt, $2. Sent post-paid by mail.

BEAUTIFUL HOMES.—DEVOTED TO HOUSE FURNISHING.—Everything relating to the picturesque furnishing of bed-room, hall, parlor, sitting-room; how to beautifully arrange all the rooms of the houses, is described. Carpets, Wash-stands, Wall-paper, the Living-Room, the Parlor, Bed-Rooms, Halls, Umbrella Stands, Door Mottoes, Toilet and Dressing Tables, Curtains, Lambrequins, Screens, the Library, Cabinets, Etageres, the Dining-Room, Window Screens and Blinds, Mantels, Chairs, Rugs, Ottomans, Tables and Stands, Sofas, Lounges, Foot Stools, Cushions, Afghans, Baskets, Racks, Tidies, Miscellaneous Conveniences, etc. Contains over 300 pages, 350 illustrations. Price, $1.50; by mail, post-paid. Gilt, $2.

EVENING AMUSEMENTS; OR HOW TO ENTERTAIN COMPANY.—A splendid book for young Ladies, Gentlemen and Children. This volume contains over 250 Games and Ways of Entertaining Company, and amusing young people at school, at parties, in home sports, picnics, for Christmas charades, tableaux, and all social occasions. Fireside Games, Tricks of Magic, Mystery, and Conjuring, Cards, Riddles, Acrostics, etc. Price, $1.50; cloth, or gilt, $2.00. Post-paid by mail.

WINDOW GARDENING.—A ready and invaluable aid to all who wish to adorn their houses in the easiest and most successful manner with plants or vines, or flowers. Instructions are given as to the best selections of plants for Baskets or Ferneries and Wardian Cases. Several chapters are devoted to Hanging Baskets, Climbing Vines, Smilax, and the Ivy, for decorative purposes. Bulbs for House Culture are fully described; also ornamental plants for Dinner Table Decoration. Other topics are well considered, such as Balcony Gardens, House-Top Gardening, Watering Plants, Home Conservatories, Fountains, Vases, Flower Stands, Soil, Air, Temperature, Propagation, Floral Boxes, the Aquarium, Rustic Conveniences for Household Ornament, and directions in detail for the general management of indoor plants for the entire year throughout the winter, spring, summer and fall. The volume contains 300 pages, and is profusely illustrated with 250 choice engravings. Price, $1.50; gilt, $2.00.

HOW TO MAKE YOUR OWN DRESSES.—PRACTICAL LECTURES ON DRESS-MAKING, with 300 Illustrations and Diagrams, by Mrs. Burdette Smith.—The design of this book is to give such plain and practical instruction in the art of Dress-making, that any lady of ordinary ability and ingenuity in the use of her scissors and needle, may, without other instruction than she finds here, become an accomplished Dressmaker. In order to make this as easy of acquirement as possible, the authoress has introduced a large number of illustrations and diagrams and these are so fully explained that a personal interview with the writer would not make the matter easier of comprehension. The Lectures embrace the whole system of plain and artistic dress-making, including dress-making for Girls and making clothes for boys, with important hints in regard to taste in dress, the selection of material and the choice of colors. Instruction is also given in various kinds Embroidery, Plain and Fancy Needle-work, Crewel-work, Lace Making, etc., etc. Price post-paid 35 cts., two copies for 60 cts.

THE PERFECT LETTER WRITER.—A complete and instructive guide for the correspondent, containing a very superior and original collection of Miscellaneous Business Letters of Application for Employment, Letters of Recommendation, Familiar and Social Correspondence, Congratulation and Condolence, Notes of Ceremony and Compliment, Rules for Conducting Public Debates and Meetings, Postal Notes and Regulations, business Laws and Maxims, Titles and Forms of Address, etc., etc. 16mo. 190 pages. Price, 30 cts.

ECONOMICAL COOK BOOK.—TEACHES HOW TO PREPARE NICE DISHES AT A MODERATE COST.—It contains over 400 carefully tried recipes, selected and arranged by a practical house-keeper. The compiler, in offering the public this volume feels that it will supply a long-felt want. These receipts are published for the benefit of those who like good plain living without incurring unnecessary expense. All directions are given in a clear concise manner. This valuable book contains 128 pages neatly bound, and is the best COOK BOOK ever published for the price, which is 30 cents post paid.

CHOICE SELECTIONS FOR AUTOGRAPH ALBUMS.—This is a book of 64 pages, with cover, and contains over 300 apt and Choice Selections and quotations in prose and poetry for Autograph Albums, Letters, Valentines, etc. It is full of wit, wisdom and tender sentiment. Price each by mail post-paid 15 cents. To Agents by the dozen post-paid 60 cents.

FROST'S LAWS AND BY-LAWS OF AMERICAN SOCIETY.—A condensed but thorough treatise of Etiquette and its usages in America. Containing plain and reliable directions for deportment on the following subjects: Letters of Introduction, Salutes and Salutations, Calls, Conversations, Invitations, Dinner Company, Balls, Morning and Evening Parties, Visiting, Street Etiquette, Riding and Driving, Traveling; Etiquette in Church, Etiquette in Places of Amusement; Servants, Hotel Etiquette, Etiquette in Weddings, Baptisms and Funerals; Etiquette with Children and at the Card Table; Visiting Cards, Letter Writing, the Ladies' Toilet, the Gentleman's Toilet; besides one hundred unclassified laws applicable to all occasions. Paper covers. Price, 30 cents.

HOW TO AMUSE AN EVENING PARTY.—A complete collection of Home Recreations, including Round Games, Forfeits, Parlor Magic, Puzzles and Comic Diversions; together with a great variety of Scientific Recreations and Evening Amusements. Profusely illustrated with nearly two hundred fine woodcuts. Here is family amusement for the million. Here is parlor or drawing room entertainment night after night for a whole winter. A young man with this volume may render himself the "beau ideal" of a delightful companion at every party. Price, 30 cents.

PAINTING ON CHINA; WHAT TO PAINT AND HOW TO PAINT IT.—A hand-book of practical instruction in Overglaze Painting, for the use of Amateurs in the Decoration of Hard Porcelain. By James C. Beard. This work affords elaborate information on all points necessary for success in the Art of China Decoration, giving a complete list of the colors especially adapted for this purpose, with their composition, showing the changes they undergo and the effect produced when subjected to the heat required for the "firing" process. It describes all the necessary appliances and explains their uses; it gives thorough instruction in the best methods adapted to simple or elaborate styles of decoration, with all the details from the commencement of a design to its final completion, with elegant specimen patterns printed in their appropriate colors.

The thoroughly practical scope of this work will be seen by an examination of its contents, each division of the work being complete, and written in a plain, familiar style, easy of comprehension and guaranteeing success.

In connection with "Firing" a description is given of the best styles of kilns or muffles, with directions for their use and management, by the aid of which the Amateur can "Fire" his own work in any stove or range.

This work is printed in the best style on fine paper, with full-page colored illustrations, and an elegant cover, executed in the most artistic manner. A beautiful small-quarto book. Illuminated flexible cover. $1.00.

DICK'S RECITATIONS AND READINGS.—No. 1. Comprising a carefully complied selection of Humorous, Pathetic, Eloquent, Patriotic and Sentimental Pieces in Poetry and Prose; exclusively designed for Recitation or Reading. Edited by William B. Dick. This is the first of a Series, uniform in size and style, which will include everything that is fresh and popular, introducing also some of the older gems of the English language that are always in demand, but excluding everything that is not eminently appropriate either for Declamation or Public Reading. Paper cover, 30 cts. Nos. 2, 3 and 4, 5, 6, 7, 8, 9. Uniform with above. Price each 30 cents.

THE ART OF DRESSING WELL.—By Miss S. A. Frost. This book is designed for ladies and gentlemen who desire to make a favorable impression upon society. Paper covers, 30 cents. Bound in boards, cloth back, 50 cents.

HOWARD'S BOOK OF LOVE-POETRY.—A curious and Beautiful Collection of Tenderly Delicate, Sweetly Pathetic and Amusingly Quizzical Poetical Love-Addresses, containing a large number of the most admired selections from the leading poets, suitable for quotations in Love Letters, and applicable to all phases and contingencies incident to the tender passion. 144 pages. Price, 25 cents.

HOWARD'S BOOK OF DRAWING ROOM THEATRICALS.—A collection of twelve short and amusing plays in one act and one scene, specially adapted for private performances; with practical directions for their preparation and management. Some of the plays are adapted for performers of one sex only. This book is just what is wanted by those who purpose getting up an entertainment of private theatricals; it contains all the necessary instructions for insuring complete success. 180 pages. Paper cover. Price, 30 cts.

NORTH'S BOOK OF LOVE-LETTERS.—With direction how to write and when to use them, and 120 Specimen Letters, suitable for Lovers of any age and condition, and under all circumstances. Interspersed with the author's comments thereon. The whole forming a convenient Handbook of valuable information and counsel for the use of those who need friendly guidance and confidential advice in matters of Love, Courtship and Marriage. By Ingoldsby North. All who wish not only to copy a love-letter, but to learn the art of writing them, will find North's book a very pleasant, sensible and friendly companion. It is an additional recommendation that the variety offered is very large. Bound in board. Price, 50 cents.

Address, PATTEN PUBLISHING COMPANY,

47 BARCLAY STREET, NEW YORK.

STAMPING OUTFIT

For Kensington and other Art Embroidery,
Outline Work, Braiding, &c.

Buy this Outfit and do your Own Stamping, and also Stamping for Others.

EACH OUTFIT CONTAINS TEN FULL SIZED
PERFORATED STAMPING PATTERNS.

The designs are, Border for Dresses and Skirts, of Rose Vine, Border of Poppies, Bunch each of Roses, Lilies, Daisies, Fuchias, Lilies of the Valley, for various kinds of Fancy Work, Outline Design of Boy and Girl, Corner Design, etc., with

FULL INSTRUCTIONS FOR STAMPING AND WORKING,

Box Stamping Powder, Distributing Pad and Brush.

This Elegant Stamping Outfit by mail, postpaid, for 60 Cents.

Extra Stamping Patterns.

Spray of Mountain Ash, 10 cents. Bunch Field Daisies, 10 cents. Bunch of Jessamine, 10 cents. Bunch of Poppy, Wheat and Corn Flower, 15 cents. Violets, 15 cents. Bunch of Wild Roses, 25 cents. Corner of Wild Roses, suitable for Table Cover or Mantel, 25 cents. Bunch Rose Buds, Jasmine and Forget-me-nots, 25 cents. Kate Greenaway Design, suitable for Splasher or Tidy, 25 cents.

All the above extra Patterns for $1.00, or the Outfit and these Patterns for $1.50 postpaid.

Box Blue Stamping Powder, 10 cents. Distributing Pad, 10 cents. Brush for Moist Stamping, 10 cents.

OUR BOOK OF 100 DESIGNS for Corners, Borders, Centers, &c., for Kensington and other Art Needlework, 25 cents. This is not a book of Working Patterns, but shows some of our Patterns in reduced size, and is a good book from which to select from. Address

PATTEN PUBLISHING CO.,
47 BARCLAY STREET, NEW YORK.

DO YOU WANT TO MAKE MONEY.

We would like an Agent in every Town

TO DO

STAMPING WITH OUR PATTERNS.

IT IS A PAYING BUSINESS.

There is no town of any size in the country in which there would not be a demand for this work. All you have to do is to let the people know that you can do stamping and have a variety of Patterns and business will begin. The Patterns can be used a thousand times and not injured, and as you get back the cost of the Pattern the first time you use it, future orders are all profit.

We give on another page a partial list of our Patterns but can furnish many other designs not mentioned. Send money in Registered letter or Postal order. Send postal stamps *only* for the fractional part of a dollar. Address all orders to

PATTEN PUBLISHING CO.,
47 BARCLAY STREET, NEW YORK.

MANUAL OF NEEDLEWORK,

EMBROIDERY, KNITTING,

CROCHETING, LACE MAKING, &c.

This is a book of over 100 Pages, giving plain and intelligent directions for doing all kinds of plain and fancy needlework, including the various kinds of artistic Embroidery, Knitting, Netting, Tatting, Crocheting, Lace Making, Darned Net Work, &c. It is profusely illustrated with cuts and diagrams showing how the various stitches are made, and is so plain and practical that it cannot fail to assist ladies in their ordinary sewing, and will also enable them to do the most **Artistic Embroidery** and to make many articles for home and personal adornment for themselves and friends.

South Kensington, Arrasene and other **new kinds of Needlework** are fully illustrated and explained, and directions giving for making many Fancy articles, including Table and Chair Scarfs, Piano Covers, Mantel and Window Lambrequins, Draperies, &c. Directions are also given for Knitting and Crocheting many useful and fancy articles. The chapter on Lace Making, will enable many ladies to make such desirable articles in Honiton and Point Lace as Collars, Collarettes, Tie Ends, Jabots, Edgings, Handkerchief Borders, Corners, &c., that will rival in beauty the most expensive lace. Macrame lace is also illustrated and explained as well as Darned net, Outline work, Rug Making, &c. We send this book postpaid for 35 cents; four for **$1.00**. Get three of your friends to send with you and obtain **Your Own Book Free.**

We will send this book and a One Dollar Outfit of STAMPING PATTERNS for $1.25.

We want Agents in all parts of the country to sell the **MANUAL OF NEEDLEWORK** and our STAMPING PATTERNS. Address

PATTEN PUBLISHING CO.,
47 BARCLAY STREET, NEW YORK.

Perforated Parchment Stamping Patterns.

---- FOR ----

Kensington Embroidery, Outline Work, Braiding, &c.

NARROW SCALLOPS.

Patterns for Flannel Embroidery, Braiding, etc. Great variety of designs! Mention what kind you want. Strips 1 to 2 inches in width, 10 cts. per strip. 2 to 4 inches in width, 15 cts. to 20 cts. per strip. Wide Scallops, 20 cts. to 30 cts. per strip.

ALPHABETS.

For Hat Bands, Napkins, Handkerchiefs, etc., etc. Alphabets, size 1 to 2 inches, 50 cts. to $1.00, per set, according to amount of work there is in the Patterns. Alphabets, 2 to 4 inches, 75 cts. to $1.25 per set. Alphabets, 4 to 6 inches, $1.00 to $2.50 per set. Single Letters, 1 to 6 inches, 10 cts. each. Large Alphabets in Outline and Braiding Designs, for Pillow Shams, Blankets, etc., etc. $2.00 to $4.00 per set, Single Letters, 20 cts. each.

NARROW KENSINGTON STRIPS.

All kinds of Designs of Flowers, Ferns, etc., etc. Mention what kind you want and what width. 1 to 2 inches wide, 10 cts. to 15 cts. per strip. 2 to 4 inches wide, 15 cts. to 20 cts. per strip. 4 to 8 inches wide, 30 cts. to 50 cts. per strip.

SMALL BOUQUETS.

For D'oylies, Pin Cushions, Perfume Bags, Handkerchiefs and one hundred other things. Designs, 1 to 3 inches square, 10 cts. each. Designs, 3 to 6 inches square, 15 cts. to 20 cts. each.

LARGE BOUQUETS.

For Tidies, Table Covers, Corners, Lambrequins, etc., etc. Designs, 6 to 10 inches square, 20 cts. to 50 cts. each.

LARGE DESIGNS.

For Table Covers, Corners, etc. Designs, 12 to 24 inches, 50 cts. to $1.00 each, according to fineness of the pattern.

A NEW CORNER DESIGN.

Rose Vine and other flowers.

UPRIGHT DESIGNS.

Eastlake Patterns, etc. A large variety of very choice designs. 25 cts. to $1.00 per strip, according to quality.

OUTLINE EMBROIDERY PATTERNS.

Small Kate Greenaway Designs, for D'oylies, Handkerchiefs, etc., etc. A fine assortment! 10 cts. to 15 cts. each. Large Kate Greenaway Designs, for Tidies, Chair Backs, etc., 20 cts. to 50 cents each. Large variety of beautiful designs!

DESIGNS FOR INFANTS' BLANKETS.

Pillow Shams, etc., Cherubs, Mottoes, Birds, Flowers, etc. etc., 75 cts. to $1.00 each.

CENTERS AND CORNERS.

For Carriage Blankets, 50 cts. to $1.00 each.

TEA TRAY SETS.

Two Sets, 75 cts. and $1.00 per set.

SINGLE FIGURES.

For Trays, Table Cloths, Side Boards, Napkins, etc., 25 cts. to 50 cts. each.

SPLASHER OUTLINE DESIGNS.

Size about 16 x 28 inches. Great variety of new designs! 65 cts. to $1.25 each. We mention a few :—Morning Dip, 75 cts. Go thou and do likewise, 75 cts. Splash! Splash! 75 cts. Caught in the Shower, $1.00. Wading Storks, 75 cts. Birds, etc., 75 cts. Pond Lilies, Swallow, etc., 75 cts. Boating in Tubs, 75 cts. "Mary, Mary, quite contrary," etc., $1.00. Æsthetic Boy and Girl, $1.00. Many other Designs.

EMBROIDERY SILK.

We will send you Embroidery Silk, any color, for 2 cts. a skein. *Shaded* Embroidery Silk comes in larger skeins, price, 3 cts. per skein. Please not send an order for *less* than 10 skeins, as it is inconvenient to send smaller quantities.

BLUE DRY STAMPING POWDER, 10 cts. per box. DISTRIBUTING PADS, 10 cts. Brush for Moist Stamping, 10 cts. Address

PATTEN PUBLISHING CO.,
47 Barclay Street, New York.

www.ingramcontent.com/pod-product-compliance
Lightning Source LLC
Chambersburg PA
CBHW021945160426
43195CB00011B/1223